HOLLYWOOD
RAT RACE

HOLLYWOOD
RAT RACE

by Edward D. Wood, Jr.

Four Walls Eight Windows
New York /London

Published in the United States by
Four Walls Eight Windows
39 West 14th Street, room 503
New York, NY 10011
http://www.fourwallseightwindows.com

U.K. offices:
Four Walls Eight Windows/Turnaround
Unit 3 Olympia Trading Estate
Coburg Road, Wood Green
London N22 6TZ

First printing December 1998.

Library of Congress Cataloguing-in-Publication Data:

Wood, Edward D., Jr.   1924-1978
   Hollywood rat race / by Edward D. Wood, Jr.
      p.   cm.
   ISBN 1-56858-119-X
   1. Acting—Vocational guidance—United States—Humor.   I. Title.
   PN2055.W66 1998
   792'.028'02373—dc21   98-45666
                                                            CIP

10 9 8 7 6 5 4 3 2 1

Printed in Canada
Text designed by Acme Art, Inc.

Although Edward D. Wood, Jr. was his legal and preferred name, the author was also known as Ed Wood, Jr., or Edw. D. Wood, Jr.

Contents

CHAPTER ONE

Hollywood and You

You became a typist for an insurance company!

You became a clerk in a department store!

You tried your hand in one of the many laundries!

You had to take a waitress job at a drive-in!

You failed as an actor or actress in Hollywood!

Some of you started in grade school or even as early as kindergarten. Perhaps it was only to dress up in Mother's clothes or put on Dad's pants, hat, and vest, but in actuality you were playing a part. It is natural in the very young to play act, to make believe.

Then later, other desires and ambitions take over. The drama teacher may have a hard time finding enough exhibitionists for the annual plays, but you are not shy. Not you! You knew you wanted to be an actor or actress more than anything else in the whole wide world. Haven't you been reading every movie magazine you could get your hands on since the time when you could only understand the pictures? Aren't you always the first to volunteer? Aren't you readily acceptable? At the outset, you get only the smaller parts—a gingerbread girl or boy in the yearly *Hansel and Gretel* or one of the group in the just as yearly *Alice in Wonderland*.

Then the following year you'd made it. You played a wicked stepfather or mother in *Hansel and Gretel*, followed by a fine job as the mean old Mad Hatter or Queen in *Alice in Wonderland*.

So sad! It seemed, even early in your career, you were destined to be the old, wretched ones. Where are the fine clothes of the lovely ladies? But all that changed the following year when you got the lead.

You've arrived. You're just wonderful. Your mom, your dad, and all your friends say so. Even your teacher, she's given you an A. (It probably should have been an E for effort.) Nothing can stand in your path now. You even played the lead in your middle-school graduation pageant.

The long summer. You read all the movie magazines—end on end of movie magazines. The stars wear those pretty clothes . . . the men are so handsome . . . the bright, wonderful smiles (courtesy of their dentists) . . . not a care in the world.

With a glow to your cheeks, with a gleam in your eyes, you proceed to high school! Now it's just a bit harder to get a part in a play, even a walk-on. You find this very difficult to figure out. You were in great demand in elementary school, why not here?

And so you ponder it until you talk to other aspiring young talents. Then you face the facts. High school is the melting pot of many grade schools and their drama classes. Your competition stronger. You must work harder and harder, even the plays are stronger and even the one-line or one-speech bits have become more difficult, as have the teachers. Then comes *Romeo and Juliet, Hamlet,* and *The Merchant of Venice*. But still you cling to your ever present movie magazine.

The glamour, the lights, the great silver screen of Hollywood. You must act! You must! You must! You must! But how? The competition has become so strong in high school that you want to cry in the hopelessness of the situation. The lines, much more difficult to learn. The teachings and direction, more demanding. It had been so easy back in grade school. Miss Ipswitch had never been this tough. And she liked you. She was a good drama teacher—she knew real talent when she saw it. But that high school drama teacher . . . what's with her? She wouldn't know talent if it jumped out of a bush and bit her.

Is this, then, a first look at what the art of acting is going to be like? More than you can possibly realize.

Acting is an art not easily practiced. *Certainly* it seemed like all fun (and no work) in the beginning. It was amusement for your friends, parents, and classmates. Now the friends, parents, and classmates are joined by outsiders—people you have never seen before, nor they you. Besides they are a paying audience and paying audiences want a little more than just you, unless you can really cut the mustard. Now mixed with friends and relatives are those who do not pat you on the head and say, "My, you were wonderful," even if you were not. There may even be a local newspaperman who finds unkind things to say. Certainly the write-ups in the school newspaper will be supercritical.

Throughout your freshman year, you've seen this happen to others, which was bit frightening to say the least. What can you do to avoid that same spot, or shall we say, spotlight.

Ahh, but then it can't happen to you. You're really good. Why you could outact any of the others with your eyes shut. Then why the fear? You've read all the classics. You've seen the best movies, even some foreign movies on the late show on television. And you've read all the movie magazines.

You walked right in and told that teacher you were good. And the teacher told you to study harder and harder and harder. You are finding that acting is not an art easily practiced. Your teacher says work and show me how good you are! Is this, then, another glimpse into the future? Isn't acting just getting on stage, or in front of a camera, and saying your lines, then going out and meeting your public to sign autographs? Wearing beautiful satins and furs at the gala openings and premieres that they show in the magazines? Must one work at acting?

In your second year there are no parts for you, you receive C grade for class work, and you realize acting is 90 percent work and study.

Next year you try it and really study harder. More study. More. Your grades go up. You get the second lead in the first play of the season, *Uncle Vanya*, a tough one to do. Your family, some strangers, even the critics are especially kind. That night at the local sweet shop, you catch your first glimpse of the great 10 percent of the business—glad-handing.

And you look ahead to the glorious future beyond, when school days and school plays are far behind and you are headed for Hollywood where you will try for a career in front of the magic eye of the movie camera. You, young lady, (young men visualize your own packing) will have your suitcases full of your high-school best: sweaters (including a good, fluffy pink angora that cost plenty), blouses, skirts, and the frilly formal you wore to the senior prom. You wonder if these will be good enough for Hollywood as you pack the old school book bag crammed with movie magazines.

You are going to get off the train at Union Station in downtown Los Angeles. Having read and reread all your movie magazines you already know what it looks like. You're going to take a taxi right to a hotel. You're going to bathe; have a good night's sleep; then next morning dress in your expensive pink angora sweater and brown skirt; grab your scrapbook (you've read this is a necessary item to show producers how good you *were*); and take the studios by storm. Here you are in Hollywood. And Hollywood is damned well going to know it.

Again the taxi comes in handy! "To the nearest studio," you grandly order. You find yourself at Columbia Pictures on Sunset Boulevard at Gower Street.

So you go! Columbia Studios!

Not a very impressive sight, it's a gray set of buildings and barnlike structures. Not very intimidating at all, even the old school buildings looked better. This will be a snap. All you have to do is walk into the casting office and wait for the receptionist, a lovely young lady (you wonder why she isn't in pictures herself) to say, "Are you represented?"

"Huh?"

"Represented? Do you have representation? An agent?"

"Well, no! I just arrived in Hollywood. I starred in our school play. I know I'll be a great star if you give me the chance. Here, look at my scrapbook." (If this receptionist has been with the studio for a year, she has gone through this same procedure and listened to the same story over a thousand times. If it's more than a year, add up the thousands.)

"Would you like to leave a picture?" she asks.

"I don't have one."

"Are you a member of SAG?"

"What's that?"

(And then you've really had it!)

"The Screen Actors Guild," she informs you.

"No!"

"Leave your name and address," she says kindly. "Honey, don't call us, we'll call you."

And you're on your way out of the studio. So what? After all, what does Columbia know about real talent, you say to yourself. You'll show them. The other studios certainly will know real talent when they see it, and they're bigger studios, too.

But you're tired after Warner Brothers, MGM, 20th Century-Fox, Paramount, and Universal Pictures, then the television studios and a rash of independent (both motion picture and television) producers, have all responded the same way.

What are you to do? Your money is running low! The hotel is very expensive. Perhaps a little room in a boarding house! Your money could last another two months that way, but can your feet? You've long since had to give up taxicabs for shank's-mare (feet) or a seat on a bus, if the producer you hope to see is absolutely too far away for walking.

Maybe all you've been told is right after all. You got your head shots, and they set you back plenty. You've left them everywhere you've been, but no one has taken a further interest. In fact, you haven't even seen a producer, or even a bona fide casting director, only receptionists and secretaries. Perhaps you do need a representative, or an agent.

So, you leave the hotel. You find a small room for fifteen dollars a week (no meals), in advance of course. A run-down, two-story place on Orange Avenue, just south of Sunset Boulevard. Strange such a dump could cost so much, but still it is better than the hotel at sixty dollars a week—that is if you can stand the silverfish in your pillows (they furnish those and possibly a cockroach or two in the middle of the night at no extra cost), and no meals. Even at that, your budget wouldn't allow for another two-month stay.

At a hock shop on Vine street you hock the hundred-dollar watch Dad gave you for graduation for ten dollars (the going exchange rate is about 10 percent). Your graduation dress and beautiful pink angora sweater bring another twenty at a second-hand ladies clothing store on Sunset Boulevard just west of Western Avenue. You've nothing left to pawn. Eating a doughnut and coffee for breakfast, skipping lunch, and having light dinner (you call it supper, perhaps) except for twice a week, you can make the two months now—just barely.

Or can you? You've got to stick it out, except a certain loneliness has set in. More shank's-mare up one side of Sunset, and down the other. Leave a picture—you're getting low on those also, and you have no more money to buy more (eight dollars a hundred, plus your resume on the back for another healthy chunk). "Don't call us, we'll call you." There are more agents in Beverly Hills, some of the very big ones. And there are more in downtown Los Angeles, the lesser ones.

Then it's all over but the phone call home. "Dad, please send me train fare." And it is really over, watch the skyline of Los Angeles as the train pulls out of Union Station where you arrived such a short time ago.

You've left the glamour capitol of the world without ever seeing a camera, except for the equipment in the windows of the camera stores on Cahuenga Boulevard.

You haven't even seen a movie star, except in the Santa Claus parade which moves up Hollywood Boulevard on Thanksgiving Eve every year (and you just happened, in your few months, to be here at that particular time).

You came, you didn't see, you didn't act. You went broke, and you left, having never made the slightest dent in the Hollywood armor. So? Where did you go wrong?

You weren't really all wrong. You started out right, right up to your graduation. You suffered the same joys and hurts, thrills and spills, even when you knew you had to work hard, harder than anybody else to get your first part in that strong high-school competition.

You did not fully realize how much stronger the competition was going to be when you arrived in Hollywood only partly prepared for it. Ten thousand newcomers a year, just like you, just as handsome or pretty, and just as talented, come to Hollywood, and all looking for the same job—yours!

Those foolish enough to come here in the first place should have enough finances to last six months or a year—prices are high in Hollywood. Three hundred to four hundred dollars a month is not unreasonable.

There are such excellent theatrical boarding and rooming houses, such as the Hollywood Studio Club (for girls only) on 1215 Lodi Place. A safe and sane way to live. Do make arrangements well in advance.

Don't kid yourself, you must have photographs. They are expensive. But they should be done by a photographer who knows his business and, knowing his business, he knows what agents and producers want to see.

The next step, after pictures, is to type, or print clearly, your name and experience, including amateur, on the back, along with your phone number (a twenty-four-hour message service is best). List your height, weight, bust, waist, and hip measurements, eye color, all sports, skills, and any unusual things you can do, and most important, your agent's name, address, and phone number.

An agent. Unless you are the luckiest of the lucky, in all probability, you will never get beyond the casting office receptionist without being represented by an agent. You wasted so much money and precious time in taxicabs, buses, and on shank's mare, traveling to studios that would never look at you. Columbia and Paramount are the only studios actually located in Hollywood (except for some television organizations). 20th Century-Fox is one block out of Beverly Hills in West Los Angeles. MGM is in Culver City. Universal is in the San Fernando valley in Universal City, and Republic is in North Hollywood.

To acquire an agent is a necessity to break into the movies, even for the smallest one-line bit. Producers won't hire an actor or actress without a SAG card. The Screen Actors Guild is a union which controls all actors and actresses from one-line wonders right up to the biggest stars in Hollywood. And SAG will not admit you without your first being signed by a producer for a film part.

Sounds like impossible, doesn't it? No job, no card—no card, no job. But it's not. Land an agent and convince him you're as good as you say you are; it'd be up to him to make it work. He'll convince a producer of your talents—he knows how. It's his business. And if he convinces the producer, and the producer will request that SAG make you a member. Remember, this is the only way to become a member. The initiation fee is two dollars, going up every year, another price to keep in mind before leaving home.

Sounds like a real problem to stick it out, doesn't it, and expensive, very expensive. It is. But you can always work nights as a waiter or waitress (about the only night work out here unless you want to drive a cab), since you must keep your days open in case of a studio or agent call.

Yet there is a much easier way: stay home. I don't mean to be as cruel as it sounds.

There is a way of avoiding the preliminaries of the Hollywood rat race for the beginner. Your early drama successes do not make you an actor or actress. Check out an excellent drama school that it is well recommended near home. But before you spend your parents' money, realize that you must work hard. There is more to being an actor or actress than getting on stage and saying a bunch of meaningless lines. Those lines are your bread and butter, suffered out by some writer, and you better understand what they say.

What is acting?

It is to portray with all your ability and sincerity a character, a *person*, with all your heart and soul.

Who is this character? Say she is a horse woman! How can you play a horse woman if you don't know the first thing about horses, or riding them?

Golf! Swimming! Diving! Tennis!

Your acting teachers can teach you the fundamentals of acting but you must find the true emotion by doing.

You're a typist—learn to type! You're a laundress—do the laundry. You're a housewife—be one! You're a nurse or a doctor—don't become a nurse or a doctor necessarily, but at least study their work.

You never know what you may be called upon to do. Acting is a demanding business and every day it becomes more demanding. It is not all satins and furs, a look at your television set any night of the week will prove that.

Feel dirt—dirty your face and hands. Hepburn, Colbert, Leigh, Davis—all your greats have won acclaim, not by being glamour girls, but by hard, hard work. The so-called glamour queens are short lived. Where are they now? Take out your old movie magazines and trace the queens of yesterday. There are a lot of yesterdays for them but no tomorrows, but then perhaps they enjoy looking at their scrapbooks. Glamour comes second. Hard work comes first.

Play baseball. Doris Day had to.

Play football. Linda Darnell had to, god rest her soul.

Fight, yes, I said, fight. Shelly Winters and Marie Windsor had to.

Ski. Claudette Colbert has to.

Learn to ride. Bette Davis had to, as a forerunner to the hundreds of Westerns being made each year for movies and television.

Swim! Esther Williams had to, as did another of the glamour queens gone into the great beyond, Marilyn Monroe.

Dance—all forms from the minuet to the potato masher. The waltz to the tango. The Charleston to the jitterbug.

Learn the fundamentals of makeup and hairstyling. Many of today's great personalities design and apply their own makeup and hairstyling.

Learn everything in your own hometown. Out here in Hollywood, learning is very expensive, and there are no friends to comfort you in time of distress. And one does not learn to ride, or do anything else, over night.

The more you know, the more you're prepared for your art and the better chance you have. Learn all you can! In the acting profession you must know something about everything. It's not easy. Don't expect it to be. But be sensible while you are learning.

Then let's say you think you have mastered your chosen trade. It is still not time to head for Hollywood. There are others who have also studied drama, and you'd only be caught up with again. Too many for too few parts. Realize how many of our young stars of today have been found in little towns across the country and the world for that matter, and how few actually are picked from the ranks of the newcomers on the streets of Hollywood.

What do you do?

Have the pictures taken by your best local photographer, using one of the hundreds of wonderful photos in movie magazine as a guide. Have several poses taken in different outfits. Try sweaters, but the really tight ones went out with the forties. Chose fluffy ones such as mohairs or angoras, ones that look expensive, even if they're not. Wear bathing suits. A dress. A suit. Select four poses from your photo proofs and have them put on a single 8 x 10 composite. Any photographer can do this for you. An agent or producer likes to see several poses but does not like to shuffle through a sheaf of photos. Have your hair set into four different styles to match the clothing worn.

Take your time. You don't have to do all the photographs in one setting. Time is what makes perfection. Don't smile all the time. Life and movies aren't like that. If you're going to be an actor or actress, get serious about it. Smile some day later at the job you've done, or while you're cashing your check at the bank. Forced smiles are phony anyway and prove nothing.

When the composite photographs are finished, have copies made, and print or type the information on the back as directed earlier in this chapter, with the one change—since you do not yet have an agent—put your own address.

A tape or record recording of your voice can also be of great help. I do not recommend a home recording because you will want top quality. Your voice may sell you. Your pictures are good, so make the recording of the same excellent quality. At this stage in your career, you can't handle the classics, so find a simple play. Study your scene. Study it! Study it! Then study it again! Find out who you are! Then record with all your heart and soul. If you are not satisfied with the results, an agent or producer won't be either, so do it over until you are.

Mail the finished photographs and recordings with an enclosed self-addressed, stamped envelope to an agent in Hollywood. Also, enclose a brief resume. Always remember, agents are on the lookout for new talent—it is their business and their life. But don't expect miracles overnight. Agents are busy, hardworking people. And if one agent doesn't give you a tumble, try another, try and try again.

You may just happen to click with one. And if you do, you're on your way. But in the meantime, you've stayed home, learned your trade among friends who want to help, and you've felt none of the hardships of waiting it out and failing as most do in a place called Hollywood. You haven't come to Hollywood, lost your finances, face, hopes, dreams, and your faith.

Complete your home study by keeping up with the action. Everyone in show business reads *Variety* or the *Hollywood Reporter*. Trade papers, we call them, and they keep us informed as to what the studios and producers are doing, in television as well as movies. Who! What! Where! When! And the Friday edition gives a complete list of pictures which are presently in production and those that are about go into production, along with the names of the main cast, director, producer, writer, and crew. Prices for subscription rates may be gotten by writing to *Daily Variety*, 6404 Sunset Boulevard, Hollywood, California and to *The Hollywood Reporter*, 6715 Sunset Boulevard, Hollywood, California.

Now, let's be optimistic. You've clicked. You have an agent, a SAG card, and a producer who is going to give you your first part.

You're in front of the cameras at last. The lights go up. The assistant director screams, "Quiet on the set!" The director says softly to the cameraman, "Roll 'em," and the camera purrs as the film passes through it. The soundman, his tape racing up to the speed the film is going through the camera, yells, "Speed!" The director looks to you and again speaks softly, so he doesn't disturb your mood. "Action." And you are acting.

Only time, then, will tell if the public welcomes you into their hearts and spends their money at the box office or not, which will make or break you, the actor or actress, who only a few short months before studied your script late into the night, got up at five, made it to the studio and in makeup and hairdressing by six, got a wardrobe fitting at seven-thirty, and was ready to shoot at eight—day in and day out! Hard work. Everyday production continued and the scenes became more complicated. Work and more work. Endless hours under the hot lights for a few fleeting moments of glamour at the premiere weeks later. Behind your bright, happy smile, the strange questions lurk: "How long will I remain a star?" "Will they like me?" and most of all, "When is my next picture?"

The most crucial concern of every actor and actress, even in the midst of shooting is "When is my next picture?"

So you want to be an actor or actress?

If you still do, you've got as good a chance as the next one and as a writer-producer-director who has given many a young actress her first chance in films, I say, "Good luck to you!"

CHAPTER TWO

I'm Ready
to Be Discovered

In my many years as a writer–producer–director, I have interviewed more than my share of beauty contest winners, would-be beauty contest winners, and phony beauty contest winners. These are girls—all girls—99 percent of whom have little more than a pretty face and figure (not disadvantages in the least), who are absolutely devoid of any actual talent.

Let's put it this way. Your school plays will mean little except that they gave you your first taste of being on stage. No matter how good you were in the school play it was only a school play, attended by your school chums, your school chum's parents, and your own relatives. Who is going to say one honest thing against your performance? Who will give an honest opinion about your talents?

Look around! Ask the others. Has anyone ever said anything but good in such a situation? Realize it for yourself. But you will inevitably continue toward Hollywood no matter what.

The first turn your newfound talents will take in quest for recognition (mainly for the girls) is some sort of beauty contest. "Mirror, mirror, on the wall. Who is the fairest of them all?"

Every day of every month of every year, somewhere there is a beauty contest for Miss Something or other and where there is a beauty contest, there is a winner, some young miss with a pretty face and figure who has the greatest possibility of missing the boat on life itself. Any town, village, or hamlet where there are enough people to vote, there is bound to be a contest for "Miss Angora Girl," "Miss Movie Theater," "Miss Cottonseed," "Miss Typewriter," "Miss Whitest Paper," Miss Sharp Toenail," and the list goes on and on, I presume, forever.

And the prizes are anything from a year's supply of toilet paper to an automobile—often from matching the "Miss" designation and sponsor—and at times, a trip to Hollywood. This usually includes a phony screen test taken in a hole-in-the-wall studio, run by associates of the character who promoted the contest in the first place. Like as not there isn't any film in the camera. It's been known to happen, quite often.

Oh, yes, all expenses are paid: second-class train ticket, a cheap motel, and a book of food tickets at a restaurant of the producer's choice. You want something extra, you pay for it out of your own pocket. You may have to pay out of your own pocket much of your so-called all expense paid trip.

Of course there are legitimate contests, and it's easy to spot them. They're publicized all over the stage, the country, and now even the world and, because of TelStar, seen almost immediately. However, even with the most extensively advertised contest, how many of the winning girls have gone on to greater glory in the movies? The beauty queen may get a picture, or two, or three, then oblivion. Perhaps she'd land a guest spot on a television quiz panel once in awhile. In case you can't remember her name, the moderator of the show will refresh your memory. The queen will be all smiles in front of the camera, until she goes backstage for a big cry. Her fame had come and gone so quickly.

How many times have you watched those girls acting and emphatically said, "Even I could do better than that." And I wouldn't doubt it. But then, what does that really mean? Better than another amateur?

Not long ago I witnessed such a talent contest in Texas. The fifty or more girls were judged solely on their good looks and artistic talents. The artistic talents consisted of anything from playing a kazoo to an attempt at swinging a baton (what baton twirling has to do with dramatic talent I have never understood) to a dramatic reading by a buxom sexy blonde. Strange as it may seem, she was the one who captured the loving cup and the trip to Hollywood. I've checked around Hollywood and can't find anyone who knows of her—I'm sure she's back in Texas by now. And remember, this was a sponsored affair. If a legitimate contest can't give talented girls a leg up, how in the world can all the gimmicky ones work?

Small contests spring up by the thousands all over the country. Local deals thought up either by local businessmen or promoted by sharpshooting con artists out for a quick buck. The individual girl is actually of little value to the man in question. He could care less who wins the contest, but somebody has to win. It's all in the game. It might as well be you. Any contest, just like a carnival or a circus, brings people to the area and people spend money with the businessmen who have sponsored the affair. The more girls in the lineup, the more parents, friends, and relatives there will be to remember the merchants long after the last gun has been fired, long after their little girl has had her first break. The men who gave it to her, the merchants, they'll be remembered. But how long the contest winner?

Let's see what our little contest winner really did get after she won the hometown beauty contest. She won, among other trinkets, a free trip, all expenses paid, to Hollywood, and a screen test.

When Mr. Producer–Promoter came to town for the beauty contest in the first place, he had to have some glorious first prize to make it interesting. His story: he's from Ipswitch Pictures in Hollywood and he has been sent out into the hinterlands looking for beautiful girls with great talent. The studio will pay for the girl to come to Hollywood to make her screen test. The businessmen of the town are only charged a small service charge, in addition to the advertising space in the official program designed and handled by the producer. It all ends up in his pockets. The minor cost of sending "Miss Whatever," the winner, to Hollywood and a few trinkets for the numerous runner-ups is negligible compared to the profits the promoter can make from this community. And the law specifies a winner must be given what was promised. The promoter certainly doesn't want to go to jail, so he pays off gladly.

The winner gets her first inkling that all is not as glorious as it was supposed to be when she arrives at the train for departure, expecting a big send-off. Oh, she is told, the promoter was called out of town unexpectedly. After all, why should he waste time on his new find? There is another town, another contest, just down the line, where he must locate another new find and another pocket full of the old green. If you think this is out of line, just ask your fellow contest winner.

So off the winner goes by chair car to Hollywood, where she is met at Union Station in downtown Los Angeles by a young lady, the "studio" representative, who gives all kinds of excuses about the absence of a greeting party. However, she promises, at the studio tomorrow, it will be different.

She takes the winner to an inexpensive motel on lower Sunset Boulevard for a restful night, again explaining the "studio owns this place" (which it doesn't), "so you understand. After all, even in big business, we have to economize. I realize it's a little shabby, but when your contract is approved by the studio your conditions will be so much better." And the contest winner certainly doesn't want to start off on the wrong foot by offending anybody.

And with busy Sunset Boulevard outside, you try to get some sleep, with the expectancy of what tomorrow will bring. After all, you might just be the one to make it.

However, tomorrow does come and there is an excited telephone call. "Our representative can't make it so you will have to take a taxi to the studio yourself—of course you'll be reimbursed for the taxi fare." (Don't you believe it. You can expect a lot of reimbursements during the next week that never seem to materialize.)

Via Yellow Cab, you arrive at the studio, an old store on Larchmont Boulevard with a few spotlights in a hastily erected living room set, an ancient 16 mm movie camera of one sort or another, and a vintage sound recorder. You are given a two-and-one-half-page script and are told, "Don't bother to memorize it and forget the makeup. We want to expose your natural beauty to the camera, and your voice should tell your own feelings—just take the script for a moment or two and tell us in your own words what you would like to say."

Then the cameraman tells you to start by saying, "Action." This must be right because you've seen it done that way in the movies. And you give your all for perhaps three full minutes—no cutting, no close ups, no changing of the camera, then, "Goodbye.

Thank you. Don't call us, we'll call you." Oh yes, on the way out you receive your book of food tickets.

What happened to the director of your test? Is the cameraman always the director? Have you always heard it wrong?

Hollywood is at your beck and call. You take a long walk on Hollywood Boulevard. Look at the bronze plaques with the names of the movie stars present and past, which lie embedded in the cement at your feet. Unless you can afford the Brown Derby or one of the restaurants on La Cienega or Upper Sunset Boulevard (they're not in your meal ticket book), you'll probably never see a movie personality close up.

Try to have a little money on hand so that you can visit a few of these places. There are many where the actors go to relax, and you can learn of them rather quickly if you put your mind to it. You'll see actors and actresses of renown at the Brown Derby in Hollywood, if you're there at the proper time. (Criswel and I even talked to the Three Stooges and Pat Butram the last time we were there.)

This walk will be about the best thing about your trip to Hollywood, unless you can afford to visit the places where the actors relax. And you're free to visit any of the studios, from the outside. Visitors inside a studio are almost unheard of. It takes practically an act of Congress to get in, except Universal International Studios in Universal City has a guided trip for a few dollars now. Also you might get a ticket to a television show at NBC or CBS, if you wait in line long enough.

You might get the idea here that everything in Hollywood is a problem. It is!

You are tired as the week passes. You haven't even been contacted by the studio representatives who brought you here in the first place, that is until the last hours of the last day. The young lady who first met you at the train arrives to take you to the station, to see you off, so to speak. She has a new load of apologies as to why you have been neglected.

"You know how busy we are at the studio these days. That's why we had to use such a small studio for your screen test. There just wasn't one inch of space left for your little test at our big ones at the major studio, with our full schedule of pictures for the theaters and an even tighter schedule of television filming. But the main thing is the test, isn't it, no matter where it was filmed? And you can rest assured it will be seen by not only the head of our studio but by all the other studios as well. Be patient, my dear. All good things take time. And again. Don't call us, we'll call you!"

Then as quickly as it had all started, it's all over. The promised glory and fame and glamour were not at all what you believed. A lost week in your life. A week in your life you can never tell the truth about. It would be so embarrassing and who would believe it. So you make up stories based on the legend of Hollywood. Stories that could well put another girl on the same road to find the same thing. The inevitable turning wheel.

No sooner have you returned home than you read in the evening papers about another beauty contest, complete with an entry blank.

What does a beauty contest really mean then? The human ego: "Mirror, mirror on the wall . . . " You enter because you're sure you are the most beautiful and have a better figure and more talent than anyone else. And if you win and you're satisfied, you'll be all the wiser. Anything else in the prize line you should take only as a matter of course. Most are of little value—even the trips—as was the Hollywood visit and the screen test. Take it for the visit and the experience, nothing more. You'll be better off in the long run. Once the contest has been completed, the promoter is absolutely finished with you. He can make no more money. He needs a new victim.

Beauty contests are entered by girls from all walks of life. Most have never considered a career as a model or an actress. I think many of the losers become even more stagestruck than the winners. The loser has to prove she should have won, and often embarks on a long, expensive jaunt to Hollywood or New York City to be a model or actress. She'll show them all up, even if it kills her, and it very well could.

Hitting the big time as a model is as improbable as it is as an actress. Just figure how many other girls, all over this big country of ours, also determine to try. Ask any lovely girl you meet on the street in New York City or Hollywood what she does for a living. And nine times out of ten her answer will be "I'm a model or actress." She is probably not making a living modeling or acting, but it sounds good and is probably what she'd like to be doing instead of working as a cocktail waitress, secretary, shop girl, until her "break" comes along. Her "break" will probably be just what drops from her serving tray.

You've heard the same thing on television interviews when the moderator asks a pretty girl that question, but then comes the moderator's next question. "What was your last picture?" And you hear her answer. "Well, I haven't made a film as yet, but I've been interviewed for such and such a picture or such and such a play or such and such a modeling agency has been thinking of signing me."

For every modeling job—whether for newcomers or professionals—there are hundreds of applicants who appear at the door. And believe me, the newcomer is the last choice, if chosen at all.

Most television advertisements that have girls washing their hair, using the washing machine, smoking some brand or other of cigarettes, or walking through the snow call for more of a model than an actress to those of us who produce. But notice how many there are. In all the ads, every minute of every day, somewhere on television, you'll find stock company arrangement of the same faces. They are tried and true. The admen have no qualms about placing these girls, even over the telephone, because they are experienced and, make no doubt about it, they never error in their delivery of lines, gestures, or whatever.

When a sponsor hopes to reach millions, he must be certain his message, whether stills or motion pictures, will be delivered and understood the way he wants it. With some great exceptions, this cannot be guaranteed by the beginner. Modeling is not just fun— it is a business into which many millions of dollars are poured each year. One into which many thousands of dollars may be spent on one 8 x 10 photograph. The advertising business must pay and pay and pay and they expect to get results from the model and her expensive sitting. The movie you see on television, the feature, may be rented for twelve hundred dollars, but the advertiser may well pay thousands of dollars for his one-minute spot, and many times that for the filming of his commercial message. He has to be sure of his model.

You say, "well others have made it, why can't I?" And I must honestly answer. "Why can't you?" But in the same breath, I repeat that the competition is so stiff that while one makes it a thousand more starve, or nearly starve. You might be the one to make it, but you probably won't.

Wanting to be a model or actress does not make you a model or actress. Even great amateur model may never get a professional chance. It takes a lot of luck no matter how much amateur experience you have.

A pretty face and figure, of course, help in many ways. But then all the top models have this and thousands of would-be and lesser-known models also are endowed with beauty of face, body, and voice.

With television—the greatest advertising medium in history—reaching masses of people at one time, we must realize the raving beauties who once dominated the magazines and billboards have been infiltrated by "Miss Plain Jane" or "Mrs. Average Housewife" or "Miss Not-So-Good-looking Schoolgirl." How can the sponsor take the pimple from a beauty with his luscious face cream? If she is already a beauty, why would she need it? Thus Miss-Not-So Beautiful sells his product best. You need to realize that with the openings for "Miss Not-So-Beautiful" there are thousands upon thousands more faces in this category to flood the already flooded market. "Miss Beauty" by the thousands. "Miss Not-So-Beautiful" by the many more thousands, all starving, side by side.

If you have definitely decided to be a model and there is no talking you out of it, try for experience in your hometown, or a town very near you so you can commute, and I don't mean the local beauty contest alone. Perhaps by winning or being a runner-up, you'll get your picture in the papers, and some doors will open a little easier for you, but then, perhaps you can open your own doors. However, don't shut those small-town doors in preference of the big cities and the bright lights. Many a top model has been discovered because her face and figure were seen advertising the products of some small-town manufacturer. Those advertisements get around more than you might realize.

I can give you an example. Those of us in the motion picture field are always interested in our competition—small companies as well as the big studios. So we go looking and investigating. You see, for each film that reaches the screen there is a publication sent to all the releasing organizations. This is called the press book, a printed brochure which tells about the film, its cast, and many ad-mats, showing the kind of posters in front of the theater to bring the customer in, as well as ad-mats for the newspapers. In all, it tells about the film and advertises the same. This is done for all films the world over. We, the producers, collect these so that we might know what is going on in our business

It is the same with the modeling agencies. They are in a position to know every person who had ever modeled for any company, big or small, in the world. They find and collect files on people working in the industry. Of course, we of the motion picture and television film companies are looking for new talent, and so are the people who employ models. Do not break down our doors! Draw our attention by doing, not telling.

The more you appear in such advertisements, the more you are likely to be remembered by an agency who has been queried by a sponsor for certain types. Remember the words "a picture is worth a thousand words." You can beat on doors all day and never get in, unless those inside want you in.

You may have all the talent there is to have. You may shout about that talent from the rooftops, but do it from your own rooftop in your own hometown where you've got the odds with you. This is true for the movie and stage aspirant, as well.

Little theaters, school plays, and hometown stagework should be seriously considered by the aspirant model also. To be seen. To get the feeling of facing an audience. You'll find the confidence you're going to need all your life no matter what you eventually do. Poise . . . grace . . . delivery.

A photograph in an advertisement can express pages of spoken words if the model can project the feeling. Stagework can be most important in giving you an insight to those feelings you may be required to give the still camera. There is nothing worse to see than a photograph with a phony or unreal laugh or smile. This is the cardinal sin of any photograph sent to me, and believe me, I've received many.

You'll find this to be fact in all phases of my business and many others. If you can't genuinely evoke an emotion, don't photograph it. For heaven sakes, if you do have it photographed, don't send it to me. Put it away somewhere in a dark corner, or a scrapbook where you can look at it years from now and say the same as I will, "Uggg."

Remember that like an actress, the first impression could very well be your last. You've got to start somewhere if you're going through with this insane career. And that somewhere is telling someone who knows you or knows of you and will listen and not be too demanding in his demands.

Face it! You're the beginner who probably hasn't begun anything but the thoughts in your own mind. However, even that is a beginning. We are looking for you! Every forward-thinking producer of films or advertising must always be on the lookout for new talent.

It would take an idiot not to realize that the life span of a model or a leading actress is approximately eight years—just after your twenties and just before your thirties. If you've got it, we want it. If you think you've got it, read the last two chapters over. . . . Hope springs eternal.

CHAPTER THREE

So You Want to Be a Star

This chapter has been needed for too long. Over the years I have seen how this particular subject of stardom has been ignored by drama teachers, would-be teachers, and glib-tongued orators professing to know the field of drama. Even an expensive book for young actors I read recently devoted no more than a six-line paragraph to the subject.

The term "character actor" refers to the men and women who are the very mainstay of all movies, television, and plays the world over. I believe it is necessary to start out your life as an actor or actress with only one thought uppermost in your mind: you will be a star.

Yet at the outset you must realize that very few can possibly achieve what is classified as star status—leading man or leading lady. But this is not to say you cannot achieve a great measure of success. Indeed the character men and women are generally longer-lived on the screen than most stars who have come and gone. Look back over the last twenty years. Which of the stars we remember are still on the scene? (And I do not include those who have gone on to the Big Movie Show in the Sky.) Not many going strong, are there? Most have become absolutely obsolete, gone, finished, lost into obscurity.

Then look back over the same twenty years at character actors. Except for those who've gone beyond, nearly every character actor who worked then is still active today and commands extremely high prices. Perhaps you can say they *are* stars in their own right—and so they are. I prefer to call them extreme experts in their chosen field! And this is what you should strive for: to be an expert. Head for the top of the character field, it can only be to your credit, and to those excellent agents, press agents, business managers, or newspaper critics and a few million fans who will decide that you're it.

(The fan business means the same to the character people as it does to the stars, and their fan mail comes in the same poundage— perhaps more poundage because there are more character people than stars. The more fan mail a studio receives for such and such a character actor or actress, the more you're going to see him or her on your screen, because the producers know they are in demand. Don't ever underestimate the power of publicity, it can make you or break you, and it can keep you on top year after year, even if you happen to get a lemon for your last script.)

Part after part, scene after scene, you've witnessed great character people like Jonathan Hale, Jane Darwell, Addison Richards, Stanley Andrews (the old ranger of television), James Burke, Allen Jenkins, Frank Scully, Rosco Ates, Iris Adrian, Barbara Pepper, Harvey B. Dunn . . . the list could go on for page after page. These people have been in hundreds of wonderful roles over the past thirty or more years and are still seen on the newest television shows. Why do they last? Because they learned their trade well.

Barbara Pepper was once a glamour queen of big musicals. Today, a bit older and a bit heavier, she is still commanding interesting parts. Who could resist or forget her radiant smile? Had she not learned the real meaning of the acting business over the years and just tried to remain a glamour girl, she'd be out of business today. But she was as intelligent as she was beautiful and her intelligence led her into the more mature roles. This classes her high in the ranks of character people and keeps her in the minds of not only the producers and directors who were her friends in the past, but of the new producers and directors of today.

Youth and beauty alone are not enough. Even talent can wear thin if it is not fed with new morsels each day. And what does it take to be a character actor or actress? The same thing as it does to be a star: a lot of study and hard work. And to be a really excellent character person, possibly a lot more.

Many of you will decide along the way to change your mind, to turn away from the acting profession. But studying acting will undoubtedly help you in whatever profession you do finally undertake because it gets out of yourself for a time. You get to be someone else. To plot with your author the fate of another person and live that other person's life.

Imagine yourself in another profession, as a salesman or a saleswoman, perhaps, who just can't seem to make it. You knock on a door. The lady of the house confronts you. You freeze. Your speech is weak. Your presentation is all wrong. Your own confidence is lacking. I doubt very much this would happen if you had had some dramatic training somewhere along the way, even if a professional acting career had never entered your mind.

This situation happened to one of my dearest and closest friends in this world. Several years ago he started his life as a salesman. There were very other few jobs in those days. He went door to door on a strict percentage basis, which is one of the toughest jobs this world has to offer. If you can't produce, there is no paycheck.

My friend was in an even more difficult position. He was frightened to death of meeting people face to face. He felt defeated before he'd even started. He was insecure about what he was selling, even though it was an excellent product and he knew it. He was insecure in his sales pitch, insecure in his presentation, his voice, and his appearance despite being a ruggedly handsome man standing well over six feet tall and sporting shoulders like the Bank of the World.

He could not deliver to the general public what he wanted to convey, no matter how much or how hard he tried. This power-house of a man was frightened to near extinction of the next potential client.

Thoroughly exasperated, he was persuaded by friends to join a drama school—as simple as that! At the school he soon found his focus, his ability to present his feelings and his inner self by living the character written for him. The character must be lived on stage and must be believed by his audience. I must emphasize that he did not go to a dramatic school to become an actor. But he improved so considerably that when he was seen in the role of the president in a play entitled *Mr. President* a motion picture studio immediately signed him. He remained under contract to them for a great many years. I'm sure my friend would not like me to say just how many years ago that was, but it was a long time ago. Since then he has been under contract at one time or another to every major studio in

Hollywood, and to the present day, rarely sees a day of unemployment. This is Roy Barcroft, one of the really great motion picture and television villains who has ever crossed the silver screen or the electronic tube—from the handsome, black-mustached villain in Buck Jones Westerns to the gray-mustached "Big Man of the Mountains" in a recent *Have Gun Will Travel* television episode.

Roy had no ambitions to be an actor. He wanted that drama school help to get ahead in his job as a salesman. He wanted to be a good salesman and strange as it might seem, Roy has been doing just that for all these years. He has been a salesman to the public as a character actor up there on the screen selling his lines. A really fine artist in the field, he continually strives to perfect. I must again say here, he certainly didn't start out in life to be either a star or even an actor, but over the years he has brought out many a hiss and sometimes a cheer from the audience, and we've loved every moment of it! The proof is that the more you want him, the more the producers want him.

Would you say Bela "Dracula" Lugosi, the greatest horror man to ever live in filmland, was a leading man? Star type, yes, but leading man? Bela Lugosi was a leading man in his native Hungary before he ever came to this country. But even there, he had to play many parts when he was at the dramatic academy. In one play, perhaps he was the lead, but then in the next, perhaps he only had a walk-on. One picture that stands out in my memory he made just before coming to this country. It was James Fenimore Cooper's *The Last of the Mohicans* and Bela played the Mohican—the character man, but the most important character in the story. Years later when the film was made in this country, the Mohican was played by Robert Barett, who was to play General MacArthur in most World War II films.

Bela Lugosi is probably one of the best examples of the character actor who made good in his career, as well as making a great deal of money in the process. To the day he died he was always in demand and I know this firsthand. My script, *Final Curtain*, which we were about to film, was found beside his bed when he died. It was opened to page six.

A personal weakness stole his fortune and his life, but never his talents. In his seventies he created the horror character on stage in *Arsenic and Old Lace* in far-off St. Louis. In the same year, he and I devised a nightclub act for the Silver Slipper in Las Vegas, which played to record-breaking audiences and was held several weeks over the original run. He also set a new record for his personal appearances at theaters.

You bet he was a character actor—with a name that will be remembered as long as there are movies or there is television.

Was Edward G. Robinson ever a leading man type? Or the excellent Walter Brennan? Or Wallace Beery? Connie Gilchrist, Kermit Maynard, Bud Osborne, Barton MacLane, Percy Kilbride, Marjorie Main, Kenne Duncan. The list goes on and on. Most of us, when we see their faces up on the screen say, "There's that fella. There's that girl. What's his name again? What's her name again?" We only know the faces, oh, but how we know those faces. The greats so successfully back up the leading man or leading lady in our favorite films.

This is the crux of this chapter: the star and the character actor of today. With a personality being exposed to the public at least once a week on television, the lead can be easily overexposed. However, the character actor, who might have been in many segments of the series, is still around. Not only around on one particular series, just switch the channel! There he is again, backing up another star in another series, then over here perhaps on a live show, or an interview—all at the same time. If you want to act, get around!

God save the character people. And since God must take us at one time or another, our business needs character actors and needs them desperately. It is up to you to decide if you are going to take this business of entertainment seriously enough to follow through, not necessarily to pursue the narrow definition of star but to follow in the great tradition of character actors.

I wonder if any of you remember the name Jack Norton?

For years, Jack Norton was the screen drunk—a character he devised, designed, and propelled to the greatest heights. Jack was never seen on the screen without his glassy eyes, bandy legs, and the comic lust for his next glass of wine, whiskey, vodka, scotch, etc. I understand in real life Jack did not partake of alcoholic beverages at all. Then how did Jack Norton become the greatest screen drunk of all time?

Jack studied every drunk he could find. New York City, Chicago, Los Angeles, Hollywood, Podunk, wherever there was a saloon Jack Norton might be seeking his next unsuspecting victim for intense study. Jack's character was a composite of the most interesting qualities usable in portraying the staggering men and women he watched.

Jack never used the hit-and-miss routine of acting. Rather he studied his subjects intellectually (without interfering with that person's private life) and decided which part of what he witnessed would apply to a character he had already accepted. Thus after long study, Jack built the character he wanted, and over the years that character was extremely kind to him. Thanks to him, a lovable character was born to us and will remain with us as long as his films are shown. On Jack's behalf, I wrote a novel called *The Inconsiderate Corpse*, and I've always been sad that Jack Norton passed into eternity before it was published and he had a chance to read it.

I cite Jack Norton as a case in point. You must observe with the idea of building a character you might someday have to, or wish to, portray. It is true that Mr. Norton made his fame and fortune, as did the great Billy "Sneeze" Gilbert, through an excellent portrayal of one specific character. But one specific character in this great age of television and mass audiences is not recommended. Of course it would not hinder your career to have a specific character to fall back on, but you should not limit yourself. I can't emphasize enough: don't limit yourself to one character!

In earlier days of the film industry, the public accepted the one image actor: Charlie Chaplin and his tramp; Snub Pollard and his drooping mustache; Ben Turpin and his crossed eyes; Wallace Beery and his lovable villainy; John Barrymore and his profile; and in later years Veronica Lake and her hair; Harold Lloyd and his glasses; Humphrey Bogart and his manliness—they all had their own trademarks. These characters were famous for a time, but it is no longer possible to succeed with just a trademark.

Remember how many years Bogart relied on the sneer before he became one of the greatest character men and won an Academy Award for *African Queen*? Even Marlon Brando had to give up his torn undershirt to progress to the great varied roles he portrays so excellently today. Take Gary Cooper. He started as the slow-drawl type. In the years that followed, he found his voice and diversified his roles. Ray Milland is an even better example. In the beginning, he favored the extremely heavy dramatic roles, but then he expanded into comedy, and later to the suspense of horror films. I wonder if Mr. Milland could have spanned all those years if he had only prepared himself to be a leading man.

The late Dick Powell was a handsome young singer in the early musicals of dubious quality that you can see on the late night or early morning movies on television. They make you wonder who would give him a chance to keep going, but he proved himself and became the finest actor–producer–director of our time.

Television proves to anyone's satisfaction that movie actors can adapt. Robert Young, television's *Father Knows Best*, was once the young lover racing up and down the beach in black-and-white shorts in a Charlie Chan movie. It stared Warner Oland as Charlie Chan and Bela Lugosi as the murder suspect and was the first Charlie Chan movie ever made in sound: *The Black Camel*.

Spanning the years, Bette Davis, Joan Crawford, and Gloria Swanson, are as great box-office draws today as ever. They are able to diversify with exactness. I'd say these stars are more than experts in their chosen fields—they are the finest character actors and actresses of our time. They must be! Look how long we have kept them on top. These people had to have *it*. And this is what you must have. You've got to have *it*. You've got to be able to grovel in the mud of life—and the mud that is thrown at you from the curb, and the mud that is thrown at you through insult—take it all and possibly you will have a chance of making it. You think they made it because they were pretty boys? Glamour girls? Perhaps for a time. And time is the big factor of all. Time, like taxes, is always there, and time takes its toll on all of us—in our faces, in our bodies. Eventually each one of you will be forced by time alone to become a character actor or actress if you are going to make drama your lifelong ambition and career.

Then why not strive for this from the very beginning? It might be hard to plan ahead twenty years—no one really likes to do that—but those twenty years will pass and it is much harder to look back over twenty years if you've lost them, or haven't gotten the most out of them.

On the set of *Mister Ed*, one of television's top shows, a young stage actor from New York singled out a man whose face he recognized from late-night television. "Ain't you Reed Howes?" asked the fellow. We hope he wasn't trying to be a wise guy, but apparently he was.

He was talking to Reed Howes, a Cecil B. De Mille find, the man who originated the fantastic stunt of standing on the wing of a speeding airplane and dropping to a motorboat in the ocean below. Howes starred in more films over a longer period than any actor I can mention. But in his later years when the pain of cancer was taking his life fast, he had to decline parts he really wanted that producers pressured him to take because he knew he could not fulfill the demanding duties. If he had to miss a day or two here and there because of his illness, he would be holding up production. So Reed became a stand-in, an extra, to make his living in the only business he knew.

On this particular day, the young fellow approached Reed. Reed turned to him, his eyes aglow at the thought that someone, anyone, had recognized him. "Why, yes. I'm Reed Howes."

The punk's seemingly friendly smile turned into a sneer. "How does it feel to be a has-been?"

Reed studied the fellow for a long moment, then said, "Don't worry, boy, you'll never be one."

As I said, Reed would not hold up production by taking a part in a film he was not sure he could complete. He was a showman.

Reed is gone now, only a year, but before he died I convinced him, with the help of his lifelong friend Kenne Duncan, a veteran of over seven-hundred-fifty films, that no matter what happened he would not be holding up production if he agreed to take a part in a film for me. Reed Howe's last feature film was *The Sinister Urge* in which he played the police commissioner. I wrote, directed, and produced the picture for Headliner Productions, Inc.

Aim for the stars and if, at the end of your life, you've only reached Mars, remember one thing. Stars flicker in and flash out. Mars is a planet. A constant light. A stable entry that will be here as long as life itself.

A character even in our own solar system!

CHAPTER FOUR

The Public Eye

So you've gone against all the advice those in the know have given you and have decided, win, lose, or draw, it's Hollywood for you. And after you've pounded the Hollywood pavements looking for recognition for a month or so it will finally dawn on you that you must have an agent if you're going to get anywhere at all. Get it imbedded into your mind now. What little chance you have of making it in the motion picture business in the first place becomes even nearer an impossibility without an agent!

An agent is also by no means easy to come by. As you'll find out, it's easier to say, "I want an agent," than it is to actually get one. Of course, an agent needs actors and actresses to stay in business but with his 10 percent commission he has to have actors and actresses who command large salaries or extremely steady jobs in order for him to make a decent living. Therefore, a newcomer couldn't possibly generate enough money to make it worthwhile for an agent to waste his time. And time is the important factor. In the same time it takes an agent to sell a producer on a newcomer, he can sell two or three of his seasoned people much easier and at far greater salaries.

Oh, it's a hard-hearted business, but a business from beginning to end. Money is the major factor in all businesses. Moviemakers are not in the business for your convenience. Moviemakers are in the business to make money. If you can be an asset to their business, they want you, but you've got to prove you can be an asset before you'll ever get a second look. I repeat: you've got to prove yourself. No one is going to prove it for you.

But look on the brighter side. There is always the possibility some agent will take a chance on you. It happens! Not often, remember, but it does happen. You must at all times be prepared for such an eventuality . . . just in case!

The composite set of photographs is a must. Your agent will in all probability sell you first to a producer using your photographs. The composite should be four photographs on a single 8 x 10 print sheet. Four photos showing you in entirely different poses and costumes as I mentioned earlier, as well as a resume. This resume should include your name, address, and a phone number, where you can be reached at all times. A message service becomes a necessity, so that no matter what time of the day or night you are called, you can be reached, and you receive your message correctly. Many a part has been lost because the actor or actress was not at the phone or did not get the message. Also on the back of the composite you should list any specialties you have. Riding, swimming, sports of any kind, typing, falls, surfing, etc. If you can do it, list it, but don't lie about what you can or can't do. You'll only be found out sooner or later and you'll end up being the loser. Be as accurate, in this, as you have ever been before in your life.

If you are some distance from Hollywood and are totally unknown to a legitimate agent, but he likes you from the composite photograph you have sent him, and he thinks you might have some possibilities, he may ask you to send him a tape recording of your voice and some form of a screen test or film to see how you photograph in movies.

If you have money enough for a paid screen test, you should seek out the best. You may have to travel to a larger city where the proper faculties are available. Again, and be convinced of this, let no one talk you into doing heavy drama. You can't handle it as this point in your career. Keep it simple! Simple! Simple! A simple scene no more than three minutes in length will be perfect.

Beware the fly-by-night screen test artist who comes to your town, in fact floods the country year after year, and I mean all towns, big and small, the country over. This is the bright, sport-jacketed, dark-glasses-wearing fellow who spots you on the street and approaches you with his calling card. The calling card informs you he is the talent scout for Ho-Hum Movie Company, Hollywood, California.

His dialogue will sound like this:

"I'm a talent scout from Ho-Hum Pictures in Hollywood, California, and I know talent when I see it and you're it." He goes on until you're practically on your way to Hollywood and the big time. There's only one hitch. He's positive you've got *it*, you're the greatest find since Harlow, but the big boys out in Hollywood gotta be shown. "Now how do we do this? After all, we can't expect a big studio like Ho-Hum to shell out money for transportation to everyone who wants to be an actress or actor. You gotta' do somethin' to show your own faith in your own career."

"What do I do?" you ask before adding, "I have always dreamed of being an actress." He's got you hooked.

"All you gotta do is make a screen test. That'll show the big shots all about you. You're bound to make a hit. Think of it! The bright lights. Your face and voice being heard all over the world like the stars you read about and see on your television and motion picture screen. Your family, your own hometown folks . . . think how you'll feel. Would you like that?"

Your answer is, of course, yes. "Oh, I would, I would, could you?" (Your words never change, year after year, no matter which of the yous you are.) Then you consent to a screen test? Of course! But how, where? And it just so happens he has a camera crew coming through for location shooting over in Hot Shot County next week.

"Now if I could only detain them a day or two so we could . . . but it's a big problem holding a crew that long, it could mean my job doing such a thing. But by golly I'll do it because you've got *it* and I'll take the chance. It could mean my job, but I'll do it. You've got *it* and I'll be darned if I let a great talent like yours get away from me. I'll have the crew stop off here for the weekend and have a real professional job done that I'll personally send off to the big shots in Hollywood. Not only that, I'll have a print made up for you. Your very own to look at when you become a big star."

Then you say, "Oh thank you Mr. So and So. How can I ever thank you enough?"

(him)

"Just sign this standard screen-test contract."

(you)

"It says here I must pay you three-hundred-fifty dollars?"

(him)

"Yeah. Just the nominal cost of film and developing. Such a small amount when you think how much I am risking. My job, my career of twenty years. Such a small investment for such a great film career ahead of you. You'll be showing the big boys what you can do and the laugh will be on them. Your talent test will actually be shot with their own studio crew. Now ain't that a laugh. Think what you can do with that at the gala parties after you're a big star."

Nine times out of ten you'll pay the three-hundred-fifty dollars. You'll appear in front of an outmoded 16 mm sound-on-film camera, in front of the director, cameraman, and his soundman (or probably all three positions will be rolled into one single man), and a set of tin flood lights against a plain backdrop. You speed through three minutes of this makeshift operation, speaking the lines you have been given. You fluff (miss) a line. You are told to continue, because it can always be corrected later. (Truth is the man won't allot any more time to you.) Time! He has a dozen more talented prospects at three-hundred-fifty dollars a pop outside the door waiting for their turn. You see, the camera crew has to be out of town that night before the sheriff from the previous town catches up with these "night riders." Your discovering talent scout has already left.

Then the facts come to light! If there was any film in the camera in the first place, the screen test will end up in your mailbox as your copy some weeks later with a short letter of assurance, on fancy stationary, that your screen test has been shipped on to "Ho-Hum Productions" and it is signed with a scribbled name and "good luck."

Had you checked first, you'd have found there was no such company as "Ho-Hum Productions" or whatever name they had given you, and that no print was ever made of your so-called screen test. If any film was exposed at all it was on 16 mm reversible and you have the only copy. But then you might get enjoyment out of the three-hundred-fifty dollars you spent over the years, if you use your screen test as a home movie. Of course, you can buy the same hundred feet of 16 mm of a Laurel and Hardy comedy for five dollars or less at the local camera store.

Unscrupulous agents work the same racket. They demand certain moneys to handle you: pay me and I'll do this for you. A legitimate agent handles you for your talent alone and will tell you at the onset whether he can represent you and what he's going to do for you. The question of money enters the conversation after you get work when the commission is ten percent of anything he lines up for you.

Before you spend any money, check the authenticity of the proposition and the propositioner.

Once an agent has graciously accepted you, you must be faithful. You must listen to him and do exactly as he tells you. All he says and does is for your own good. He can't make money unless you do, so even if something seems silly, obey your agent without hesitation. He can make you a star, if you have the talent. And talent isn't always the main factor. Your agent has all the advantages at his fingertips.

Heed his word. If you're starving for a part but your agent says no, you don't accept it. He has his reasons and doesn't have the time to go into long explanations. Perhaps the part was not right for you as a beginner and could do you more harm than good. He knows your character, he knows what he has told the producer, he knows how to climb each rung on the ladder. He has to, you're his living.

You must always be on call. Hollywood is an all-day, all-night town. Many an actress has lost out completely with an agent, producer, assistant director, or director, because she was just too sleepy to meet him at a local restaurant after he has just met some producer at two AM. It's worth repeating: Hollywood's an all-day, all-night town.

Figure it this way. The producer or the director has been tied up all day on the set. Two AM over a roast beef and cheese sandwich is the only time your agent could get to him, and you'd better be on your way when he calls.

This harkens back to the importance of the message service. Since you cannot be sitting at home in your bed in your fluffy marabou negligee, every minute of every day and night, and you certainly can't carry your telephone around in your pocket or purse, you've got to know your messages will get to you. There are many phone services at extremely reasonable rates. A twenty-four-hour continuous message service is a must.

The assistant director who gives out the calls for the actor or actress to be used the following day may not know who is scheduled until he is informed by the director, who can't possibly know himself until the day's shooting is finished. It's likely filming will not end until late in the evening, or the wee hours of the morning, at which time you are perhaps at dinner, or some social gathering. To miss a studio call is a cardinal sin, a sin for which there is no forgiveness. Your agent will insist on a guarantee that you can be reached at all times.

Your next problem will be the right kind of well-directed publicity. No matter how long you live or how long you retain you status as a actor or actress, it will cost you good hard cash for your publicity and a never-ending succession of press releases and publicity statements. Your last bit of publicity is as dead as yesterday's newspaper. There must be new releases every few days—every day if possible—not only getting your name in the papers, but also interesting your public in what you are doing and are about to be doing. Some of the stories are contrived, of course, but you're only as good as your last press release. (I recently generated press releases for a mayoralty race and we turned out as many as ten-thousand words a day in press releases to elect the mayor.) It is well known that you are only as good as your press agent paints you to be and many a star owes his or her success to the press agent.

Once you are accepted into the business your public image becomes extremely important and extremely exaggerated beyond your wildest imagination. You have read in the fan magazines about your favorite personality, both good and bad, but you never have realized the subtle messages you have been given in the text. Covertly, you have been encouraged to like or dislike certain personalities—to make this one a star or to reject that one. Put yourself in that place—you are the one to be accepted or rejected. You are the one others read about and remember. The studios and other producers read also, and you will find that you no longer have private life, as long as you are in the public eye.

The public eye is a monster of the world which will scope you from your very first entrance onto the stage to your final curtain. From where you were to where you're going, what time you get up to what time you go to bed. Even the brand of ketchup you use on your cheeseburger at the local drive-in will come under scrutiny, though you may not remember the brand yourself. When you are in the grasp of the greatest monster of all times—the public eye— nothing is too nit-picking to be magnified for the good, the bad, the indifferent.

As an example, say a run-of-the-mill man has too much to drink at his local cocktail lounge. He staggers out onto the street where a policeman spots him and locks him up in the jail house overnight, "for his own good." The story may appear, if at all, in a small article in the back pages of the *Los Angeles Times* or the *Los Angeles Herald-Examiner.*

A man or woman in this predicament, which happens thousands of times a day all over the country, is taken to jail and is booked for his or her offense. However, while being booked, the person must tell his or her occupation. Just say you're an actress or an actor, you are no longer jailed "for your own good," instead your offense has mushroomed into a major crime to be dealt with severely, and your name appears as a headline, not only in the *Los Angeles Times* and the *Los Angeles Herald-Examiner,* but in every newspaper and magazine across the country, the world. Those same headlines are magnified in your own hometown!

I've often wondered how many of you have taken into consideration what the simple word publicity really means.

It was great to see your name in the grade school, high school, or local papers, when you appeared in a play. No one ever says anything bad about you in local papers, it just doesn't happen. Think now how it would appear if, as a Hollywood actor or actress, you were involved in an automobile accident, or some other, minor incident. Now you are dominated by the all-seeing public eye, and the problem intensifies, magnifies, until you are a violent problem to the community and to the world.

Both your agent and your publicity representative are your father confessors. Perhaps you do have some problem of a personal nature. They'd better know about it right from the start. They know the reporters who are going to make their living by reporting about you. You'd better have an excellent publicity man on your side. If you've had a bad review in a recent film, it's your publicity agent who will be able to soften the blow in future articles.

Let's get back to the point: you'd better listen to your agent!

Your agent will also tell you what to wear and at what time of the day to wear it, including exactly what to wear at any particular interview with a particular producer or director. He knows their tastes and as a general rule, he knows the part he has you up for and just what the character, you, should look like. Many a producer or casting director can't see beyond the end of their nose. The more you look the part, the better chance you have.

Again money plays an important part in your career. You may not have the required clothing, but if you've got the available cash you can buy or rent the necessary items. Or if you've been around town long enough (and believe me, you will have, before you even get a chance at a part or interview), you'll have made some friends and can borrow the needed items.

You're in Hollywood, so look like it. You've got to have the Hollywood appearance on dates, out shopping, anywhere. Look the part, so in advance be prepared to pay in advance for it!

Why is this so important? To impress people, of course! For every acting part there will be dozens, perhaps hundreds in line. You must be the one to stand out above all the others. And how in the world do you expect to a newcomer to get in if you are not instantly impressive?

Your father confessor agent will do most of your legwork and he'll line up jobs for you but the first impression you make could be your last.

A very dear friend of mine who passed away only a few short months ago was one of the all-time great screen villains, Bud Osborne.

During his lifetime, Bud played the part of the villain in twelve hundred or more Westerns, from before the days of William S. Hart, right up to the present television Westerns. Yet once not long ago, Bud went to a studio where he had made hundreds of pictures over the years. They were casting the part of Frank Buck, in the serial of the same name. Bud had many of the features appropriate for the great jungle man. Bud, dressed in his most rugged western attire, approached the producer, who happened to be a theater producer from New York who was unfamiliar character people— he took a person only at face value. What he saw in front of him at that moment was a cowboy, nothing more.

"Sure," said the producer. "I know you, Mr. Osborne, know all your work, but you're just not the right type for the part. You're a cowboy actor."

Later, Bud's agent blew his top. The agent had been on the scene nearly every day for a month trying to land Bud that part. In another day or so he would have had Bud appear before the producer, but certainly not dressed in western attire.

However, there is a happy ending to the story as most of you Saturday afternoon serial watchers know. The producer granted Bud another interview and Bud appeared in a pith helmet and khakis. Despite going over his agent's head, Bud became Frank Buck and had a job that lasted many weeks.

Veteran though he was, Bud had been typed in the producer's mind, even with his fifty or more years in the movie business. He had to prove himself as an actor who could undertake any role.

Most times a producer and casting director can't see beyond the end of their noses. An actor or actress is established as one type and as far as the producer is concerned, that's all the actor can do, unless the producer can be convinced otherwise. Your agent is the best source for advice on the exact way to accomplish this.

I must confess, there was a time when I first started in the film industry in 1951, when I was opinionated. But I was lucky. My first film, *Crossroad Avenger*, was a Western. I cast all cowboy types with the exception of one, Lyle Talbot. The film starred Tom Keene and Tom Tyler. But even then, I knew fine actors could also be fine Western actors. John Carradine certainly proved it in the award-winning *Stagecoach*. Thus I cast Lyle Talbot as the lead villain in my Western. Mr. Talbot turned in a tremendous performance and has since worked with me in several more of my films, as a psychiatrist in *Jailbait*, a police inspector in *Behind Locked Doors*, a general in *Plan 9 from Outer Space,* as well as many roles. Mr. Talbot is a polished actor, a man who should be able to take any part turn in a great performance.

In *Crossroad Avenger*, I used Bud Osborne as Mr. Talbot's right-hand trigger man. This was a snap for Bud, he was in a role he'd been comfortable in for more than half a century. However in ensuing years, I had Bud eaten by an octopus, murdered by a mad occultist, terrorized by a screaming skull, beaten to death by gangsters, and opposing Bela Lugosi in *Bride of the Monster*. You must prove to be ready for any and everything you are called upon to do. It will be years—if ever—before you can pick and choose your own parts.

It doesn't hurt to emphasize once more the high cost of living and the high cost of attempting to be an actor or actress! From the moment you step out your front door it's going to start costing you money. Every move you make and every breath you take will be measured in cold, hard cash. For a long time it will be all outgoing with little or no incoming, at least from acting.

Your agent, if you get one, makes no money unless you do. If he asks you for any up front, get rid of him. He's a phony and will do you no good anyway. But by the same token, you can't expect your agent to pay your way. Those composite pictures are going to set you back an immediate two hundred and fifty dollars or more. Your wardrobe, many times that, and your publicity representative does not work on a commission. Your rent is pricey and the landlord doesn't care what business you're in—he's seen too many of you come and go. And he has a lead ear as far as how great an actor or actress you'll be someday. And you've got to eat. Like as not you'll have to take a nighttime job just to survive, let alone pay the extras which will become necessary. At the same time you're learning your drama lessons, better learn also to be a good waitress or typist, waiter or parking lot attendant. It will become as important to you as anything you ever hope to do in your selected career. It has a paycheck every Friday afternoon.

The road to any dream, to make that dream a reality, is a tough road. Dreams can only become a reality if you face facts. Face them squarely and realize all those around you have their dreams also. Perhaps you may have to dream a little deeper!

CHAPTER FIVE

Thrills and Spills

An incident on the set only yesterday—an almost fatal disaster—embellishes one of my favorite subjects. Never outright lie. Never cheat even yourself. What have you gained by lying or cheating? Some measure of feigned success? And even that, for how long?

Most of us in the business for any length of time can see through a foliage of lies, but any of us in the heat of production are liable to be taken in. So when could John Carpenter—himself one of the finest horsemen ever to cross your silver screen and the producer and director of *The Tender and the Wild* (soon to be screened in theaters all over the world)—get time to investigate everyone who comes to him, or is brought to him on good authority? I'd say the director of a Western is the most harassed person in the industry. And if that director is also the producer, it's possible he might get one full night's sleep during an entire production.

Thus a young fellow, not yet out of his teens, became acquainted with the friend of a friend who knew an independent producer, and as it happened that producer–director was about to make *The Tender and the Wild.* The fellow was thrilled. All his young life he had gone to cowboy pictures, watched *Bonanza, Gunsmoke, Wyatt Earp,* and all the other Westerns on television. He just had to dress up like "them thar" cowboys. He just had to get into cowboy pictures no matter what he had to do or say.

And now this friend of a friend of a friend was going to get him an interview with John Carpenter. Interview be damned. He'd agree to do anything anybody asked him to do. After the meeting, the fellow hounded Mr. Carpenter day after day until the producer finally gave in and gave him a one-line bit.

The boy, dressed like a gunfighter of the Old West (Wyatt Earp style), appeared on the set bright and early and wide-eyed with anticipation for the first day of shooting. He waited around most of the day until he was called. It was a simple shot. The director had to dirty him down to appear more like the outlaw he was to portray, then the boy was to be in the outlaw gang as they crawled through the dust and stormed a fort, killing off all the soldiers. During the gunfight the boy was to yell, "I got two of 'em" and his part was finished.

But would you be satisfied with such a small bit, especially in your first film, although of course each and every one of you will swear, "Just let me in the door, just let me walk in front of the camera and I'll be happy." Don't you believe it. It doesn't work that way.

When and if you get the first walk-through part it will only act as a heavy drug on you. You've got to have more and more and more. So it was with this young fellow.

He had played out his line, and technically he was through with the film. He could go home. Instead he preferred to remain on the set and at every turn he was in the director's hair, pestering him for more scenes. Just one more line. He'd do anything.

Until out of sheer exhaustion, the director gave in and asked the boy if he could ride. Of course, he could ride, he answered. He was the best. Didn't he do it every day in his hometown of Brooklyn? Hadn't he watched the cowboys ride all his young life?

Did he ever do a stunt fall from a racing horse? Of course, he had. Didn't he do it every day in his hometown of Brooklyn?

After all he was no amateur to movies. He'd been at it all of seven hours. Up to this point the boy was just another in a long line of actors, although this young lad had handled his one-line bit quite well. He had crawled through the dirt and the mud with no complaints.

In the next scene to be shot, the hero throws several sticks of dynamite at a bar. The pre-set charges go off, blasting dirt and woodwork all over the set. As the dust settles the barn doors fly open and thirty-six riders race out to meet the hero's rapid-fire shooting. Horses go in all directions. Powder dust fills the air. Professional stunt riders fall from their horses—and here is where the young fellow became involved.

Since in reality he could do little more than climb into the saddle, he figured he could stay out of the way by being last out of the barn. In *front* of the stampeding professionals, he could get into trouble. A grave mistake.

Had he been in the lead, he could have picked his spot to fall. As it was, he rode his horse right into the spinning, bucking, speeding mass of men and horses. A rifle went off under the horse's nose. The horse kicked, then bucked and hit another spinning horse and rider. The boy was toppled from the saddle, with his right foot firmly embedded in the stirrup. The horse took off at breakneck speed with the hapless, helpless boy bouncing between the racing hooves and the hard ground. The horse shot to the left to miss the corral, but the boy didn't miss it. His free, swinging body crashed through three rails of the fence, then swung around to smash down a giant endpost. Still his foot held steadfast in the stirrup.

The camera stopped. Cast and crew charged through the set; screams came from all directions, except from the boy. The horse raced on another six or more hundred yards to a point where it slammed the young fellow beneath the iron wheels of a stationary old-time water wagon. At this point the saddle tore loose and the boy's unconscious body finally came to rest, stilled, in the alkali dust.

Death had visited the set that day, but walked away without a victim. The boy had been lucky. He hadn't been killed. But for many weeks, perhaps even months, there will be times he'll wish he had been. The easiest part for him came near the beginning, just after he had fallen from the saddle. The horse's hoof put a ten-inch gash in the side of his head and rendered him unconscious, so for the next horrifying moments, he felt no pain.

He had broken his left arm and right leg, also twisted that leg out of its socket at the knee, broken his right ankle, fractured multiple ribs, and bruised and cut his entire body, as well as injuring his head.

Someday he'll probably ride again. Maybe someday those in power will even give him another chance in front of the cameras, that is if they forget he was the guy who bragged how good he was and cost the company large amounts of money in hospitalization, lawsuit settlements, and great damage to the big scene.

This is not an isolated case. Such things happen every week.

An Indian on the set observed after the boy had come to consciousness, "That's the name of the game, Sonny. Thrills and spills. If you're after the thrills, you gotta take the spills. And if you can't go that way, take off the big hat and head for home."

Sure when your first break comes along you'd do anything to please. Say yes to everybody and everything. You could, however, "yes" yourself right out of the business, or as in this story, "yes" yourself right into the hospital, or even the grave as many grieving relatives can tell you.

If you're given a chance, don't bite off more than you can chew. Don't be afraid to admit it when you can't handle some situation. But don't get me wrong if you can handle it, say so. Your producer or director will thank you because you'll be saving them time and money. But if you can't handle the scene and say you can, the whole thing has to be done over. Time and money. It makes you as bad and as harmful as a hard-to-get-along-with actor.

In some cases, experience is the most important preparation for acting. I must take you back to a period before the turn of this century, to the great cattle drives of the Southwest and the Chisholm Trail. My late friend Bud Osborne was a young fellow, actually a cowboy, herding the cattle on that trail. In fact, he even drove the last herd along the Chisholm Trail before the railroads took over. Bud drove horses and stagecoaches with two, four, and six horses—for real—it was no movie set, no make believe. This was his living. He knew what he was doing.

And so when motion pictures came into being and Westerns rose to great popularity, it became a necessity for producers to seek out men who knew how to ride, rope, and drive the various horse-drawn vehicles at the high rates of speed demanded by audiences of action pictures. Obviously, these men needed the skill to do these fast-action scenes without getting themselves killed.

The famous 101 Ranch produced many heroes of those early films, heroes we still watch on television. Buck Jones, Tom Mix, and of course Bud Osborne.

One just doesn't walk on set one day and say, "Sure, I'm a stagecoach driver." But Bud drove stagecoaches, coaches of every kind, for more than sixty years of his movie career. Remember the great race between a railroad train (the Iron Horse) and a stagecoach in Errol Flynn's *Dodge City?* That was Bud Osborne holding the ribbons of that coach. What a race that was, maybe the stagecoach didn't win against the Iron Horse but it sure gave it a great run for its money with Bud driving.

It took more than sixty years and a lot of miles, motion picture footage, knocks, bruises, and broken bones, to become the artist he was. I believe there is no one on the face of this earth who can say Bud Osborne was not an expert. Bud was the expert of all experts, only equaled by Roy Barcroft, Yackima Cannt, George Cheeseboro, and Wally Wales. Again, all of them are character men who have had the knocks and bruises to make them perfectionists.

It isn't always the actor who is at fault. In the case of Bud's first picture, it was a combination of an inexperienced actor and a director inexperienced in motion picture techniques. This director was hired to do a Western but had never done one and wouldn't listen to anyone who had.

For some reason one of the major studios saw fit to hire a young New York stage director and put him to work directing a Western film. Why? I don't know. All those I've talked to over the years haven't come up with an answer. Anyway, he got the job. And Bud Orborne was hired as the stagecoach driver. A small speaking part, but the part was instrumental since Bud was the driver in the crucial speeding stagecoach scene in which he had to negotiate treacherous conditions and his six horses.

The director described what he wanted.

"Bud, take the coach up to that ridge. When I give you action, slam those horses up and streak across the top of the ridge, then pull them hard down the grade and do a ninety-degree turn around that rock over there."

Bud interrupted.

"You got six actors in that coach."

"So?"

"How many of 'em you want killed?"

The director was stunned at his authority being questioned.

But Bud continued. "Drivin' a team of six horses at breakneck speed round a ninety-degree cut, nobody makes a ninety-degree turn at that kinda speed and stays right side up."

"Perhaps, Mr. Osborne, we should get someone else to drive the coach!"

"Better make it an ambulance driver cause somebody's gonna need him."

Nobody was going have the last line on this director. "And they tell me you're the best six-up driver in the business."

"And I figure to remain just that and all in one piece."

"Turn in your outfit to the wardrobe department."

Bud did just that. He turned in his leather vest, checked shirt, buckskin trousers, and gray cowboy hat to the wardrobe trailer on location, got into his Rambler station wagon, and drove home.

The dust from Bud's departure had barely settled before an actor brought out from the New York stage by his director friend stepped up and took Bud's place on the seat of the stagecoach. HE whipped the horses into action, the camera ground out the film, and the picture you can see at your local theater.

What you will not see is the coach as it hit the rock, turned over, and splintered into a thousand pieces. How a girl was killed and how the young actor who had taken Bud's place settled for a broken arm, a broken leg, and multiple rib fractures (he was able to dive off the driver's seat as the coach went over). Or how two of the six horses were so maimed they had to be destroyed to put them out of their misery. How the others in the coach had to be hospitalized, how the company had to be dismissed for several days, how the director was fired, and how Bud was asked to return and finish the scene.

Not a very happy ending. It seems all films must have a happy ending whether it's on the big screen, wide screen, cinemascope, panovision, or television. This film also had a general happy ending. An expert who had driven stampeding horses on the Chisholm Trail had told them it couldn't be done. Bud walked off the job because it couldn't be done the way the director wanted. Bud was rehired after the accident and the picture ended (with its new director) as the script specified. The young actor who had taken Bud's lines but not his advice learned, nearly too late, that he had bitten off a lot more than he could chew. He found it would take him a good many years to be a Bud Osborne—if ever.

Bud returned to do the scene, on his own terms: a speed the movie public would enjoy, but a speed that Bud knew the coach, the horses, and his passengers could endure.

You need to know your strengths and limitations even when your part doesn't call for danger. In times gone by an actor or an actress was given a screen test to see how they photograph before they were ever assigned to a role. Today, just as often as not, if a young actor or actress is selected for a part they will see the camera for the first time when they are about to do their bit. What a horror to many when they see themselves on the screen for the first time only to find out they are not at all photogenic. The still camera made them look handsome or ravishing, but when pictures move, things happen that even the cleverest makeup man may not be able to do anything about. Instantly the camera adds ten to fifteen pounds and the wider the screen, the heavier the poundage.

I refer to the little screen test I suggested you can do. At least you can pretty well tell what you will look like when the pictures move—and so will your proposed producer.

There was a ravishingly beautiful blonde model, who was far up the ladder in the field of modeling, but who always wanted to be in pictures. Her chance came. It was a bit in a horror flick with Bela Lugosi. When the picture was screened, Bela arrived in the dark projection booth sometime after the picture had started and sat down not knowing the girl was present. Being an outspoken man, he viewed the girl's part and commented, "Ven vat girl valks across the screen she looks like a vet dishrag." I'm afraid she did. The beauty in stills was a hag on the moving screen. The girl left the projection room, and from what I understand, never appeared in another film. Of course, the scene had to be reshot.

But try to imagine the great expense undertaken just to correct this small, but major scene: rehiring the crew, bringing back actors who had already been released—worse case scenario is that the needed actors might already be tied up on another assignment, causing another costly delay—and rebuilding the sets. It's not easy to reshoot a scene once the picture has been completed.

Acting is as much a trade as anything else in this world, so learn it as much as you possibly can before attempting to make a living at it. Just like a shoemaker, a baker, or a candlestick maker! A shoemaker certainly wouldn't go into business without an apprenticeship. If he did, he wouldn't be in business long. And the same thing applies to the candlestick maker or the baker. Remember how your first cake tasted, the one you baked just by reading the directions? You certainly went about finding out how it's done before you tried the next one. You probably became an apprentice to your mother.

The atomic bomb didn't just happen. Many people of many trades, skilled people of long apprenticeship and longer study were commissioned for such a magnificent undertaking. Of the hundreds of thousands or perhaps millions of people who would have liked to work on such a project, the men and women whose names you read in the newspapers were chosen because they have their trade well in hand. They knew it and they lived it, they are their trade. Just imagine what would happen if one person were permitted to cut in line, got the job, but couldn't handle it. He makes an error and the scene is spoiled. I wonder how we'd reshoot the atomic bomb dropping.

Far-fetched? Think about it!

Certainly, every year someone bluffs his or her way into the film business. We, the producers, are not infallible. We can be misled and hire someone totally unsuited only to discover our mistake when we view the rushes in the projection room. Rushes refers to the film of the scene or scenes shot the day before and seen by those in power. The powers-that-be are usually the producer, director, first and second assistant directors, script girl, secretary, cameraman, and film editor. Very seldom, and I repeat, very seldom the star or stars of the show might be there in the darkness. Most stars refuse to see themselves in rushes, it might frighten them so much they'd quit the business. It is reported that George Raft has never even seen any of his pictures after all these years, let alone the rushes on them.

The sound for rushes is on magnetic tape at this time and the picture is on the film. The two pieces run through their respective vehicles in synchronization so that we can see and hear everything, but there are no sound effects or music to enhance the scene. Many times I have witnessed an actor getting an award and wondered how the award committee would react to the rushes of that performance, where there was no help from the specially designed sound and music effects.

It is generally the rushes that indicate the errors of ourselves and others. However, alas, we may be very tired one night, or turn to discuss something at the wrong time and something escapes even our trained eyes. But more errors are found at this point. Rushes are no-holds-barred. They tell all. The camera doesn't lie.

The rushes tell how good you are, providing you've made it this far. And while you might lie, the camera does not. It is here you've got a chance or a flat rejection. It's here you are easily replaced. Even if you have a contract for the run of the picture, although this is unheard-of for the beginner, all the producer has to do is pay off the contract, discard the film, and reshoot the scenes tomorrow with someone else. He's getting off cheap since he found the error of *your* ways before the sets have been struck or the picture completed.

If you're finished in the rushes, look how many people on that one picture saw and heard the report. And each of those people will go his or her own way to many films and to many listening ears. You try bluffing your way and you've had it. Hollywood is a small place.

The strange thing about this is, even though the boy on the horse will probably never work professionally again, we all remember his name. His fall was one of the most sensational the producer ever had in his career.

Think. Use common sense. Be a secretary, an engineer, a butcher, or a baker. You will find your niche in this crazy world of ours whether it be movies, television, stage, modeling, or just the world!

CHAPTER SIX

How to
Live in Hollywood
without Money

It's not easy, but it's possible to live in Hollywood without any money, if you are a certain type of person. If you go at it with purpose and determination.

This is the toughest business in the universe in which to get a start. Coming to Hollywood doesn't necessarily mean you'll ever see the inside of a motion picture or television studio unless you take the Tanner tour bus, or the tour of the Universal lot in Universal City. At least there, because of Universal's ever-increasing television production, you might catch some actual scenes being shot, and with the greatest of luck, you might get to see Herman Munster on his way to work.

But no matter how many of us have gone up the trail ahead of you and tell you to stay home and forget it, many of you will still head to the ever-congested Hollywood. Actually I was no different eighteen years ago. I read all the articles I could find about Hollywood and what it took to get ahead. I questioned anyone who had been there and they advised me the way I am advising you.

Just about all the advice went in one ear and out the other. I still came to Hollywood.

And I found myself *very* broke in a *very* short time, and in a *very* unfriendly town. As you will.

Over these last eighteen years, I've found that most people involved creatively in the entertainment industry entered the film capital of the world to be an actor or actress. And it's not that most of them failed. Take the wonderful Ida Lupino. A great actress first, now a fine producer and director. The late Dick Powell was not only a fine actor and producer and director, but an extremely successful business executive. Lucille Ball and Desi Arnaz can do it all. The list goes on and on, almost endlessly, with a great many giving up their acting careers, or at least limiting their appearances to minor guest shots. It is more important to the intelligent person who wishes to stay in the entertainment field to have their sights set on more than one facet of the business.

During the movie's heyday of the 1930s and early 1940s, a great number of stars specialized in Westerns. Tom Keene, a handsome, college-educated man chosen by Cecil B. DeMille to lead in one of his last silent films, *Godless Girl*, was one of the top five. Tom became Paramount's leading Western star, later moving over to RKO, then on to the old Monogram lot where his star remained until the war years. Like most of us, he joined up with Uncle Sam and the war effort. He was a movie hero on the screen, but he was a true-to-life hero in the South Pacific.

Upon returning to movie life, Tom found the entire outlook of the industry completely changed. The importance of television was about to be realized. Studios, not certain of their own future, were closing their doors and production as we knew it was a thing of the past. Independent motion picture producers emerged. The independent producer is one who has or can raise the money to produce a film without the backing of a major studio. Usually on short budgets and working with lesser-known actors and actresses, the independent producer has no studio, so he rents space for the duration of his production. When the film is shot, if it's good enough, a releasing company will distribute it on a percentage basis. If it's not any good—and you'd be surprised to know how many achieve this dubious status—the film goes "on the shelf," meaning it is never released and never seen by the public. This becomes a total loss to the producer and investor alike.

Independent producers fall by the wayside with every passing breeze just as rashes of new actors and actresses' names appear on marquees without remaining there for long.

The Saturday afternoon cowboy picture has been lost to the ages. Clouds of a past day include the hero with the tall white hat and his ever-present white horse; the villain with his black hat and black horse; the simple story about Miss Nancy and her father whose ranch is being stolen or the stagecoach holdups about to put the stagecoach line out of business; the sheriff who has to rid his town of the outlaws.

The man's entire life and his study had been devoted to his screen hero status, but Tom had to find new outlets for his great personality, ability, and talents. He prepared and took the city and state examinations to be licensed in real estate and insurance. Tom became one of Beverly Hills' foremost insurance men.

Ironically, it *wasn't* that Tom couldn't change with the tide, it was the Western itself that changed so fantastically. The cowboy film was no longer a cowboy film, it was a "Western." It wasn't a clear battle between hero and villain, good and evil. Now the hero had to have doubts about his achievements. Everyone needed a dose of neurosis and to be up to their ears in Freudian, subconscious problems.

Tom could have done it, you could say, if the writer gave him the lines. After all, Tom was an actor and he should have been able to deliver.

Back in the 1930s, the national Parent Teacher Association awarded Tom Keene plaques, statues, and documents proclaiming the purity and perfection of his diction. In addition, Tom never used an offensive work on screen in his entire career. With the advent of the angst-filled Western, the writers were punctuating their screenplays with raw language—in Tom's book, offensive words. So, Tom's era was over, the present Western didn't need or want his eloquence of voice or speech. Tom decided he had too many fans and too much of a reputation to change his image, so he went elsewhere. He preserved his image to the end of his life.

Not that he quit the film business for good. Because he didn't.

On March 21, 1951, I became instrumental in Tom Keene's life. An avid fan since the 1930s, I was about to coproduce (with Beverly Hills attorney Lew Dubin) and direct a film I'd written. I sought Tom out to star, with the late Tom Tyler, in *Crossroad Avenger*. Keene wore the white hat and was called the Tucson Kid. He was back in the saddle because he was able to occupy it the way he always had and maintain the image he had always guarded.

Tom Keene kept his insurance agency to the day he died. In his last few years, he played the sheriff in TV's *Sky King*, then went back to his insurance business. Then he did *The Last of the Heroes* with Roy Rogers, then back to the insurance game, then a commercial for the telephone company, then *The Gunslinger*, *War Dance*, and *Double Noose*, all of which I wrote.

Then he started turning down parts. Apparently, he was getting tired. I never realized, at the time, just how tired he was getting because Tom was never one to complain. He was tempted back into acting by a starring role as the army colonel in my *Plan 9 from Outer Space*. Tom Keene left this world on August 5, 1963.

After 1957, Tom wasn't interested in continuing an acting career. He returned to the screen because he was my friend, but nothing was as important to him as his insurance business. What do you suppose would have happened to him had he not discovered another way to make a living?

Even those actors and actresses who have at one time managed some level of success are not as lucky as Tom. Most haven't the slightest idea how to make a living at anything else. And in addition to making a living, you may need to make an investment in your career. Just about all the little theater groups in the Hollywood-Los Angeles area charge you money to appear on their stage. It's a living for the little theater owner. Good, bad, or indifferent, you can be cast by one of these little theater groups if you can afford the fee. The Los Angeles newspapers carry ads every day for them. But as they will assure you not to forget, if you pay your fee and appear on the stage you will be seen by agents, talent scouts, producers, and directors.

With one major exception and problem! The agents, talent scouts, producers, and directors seem to be conveniently out of town the night your play is appearing. And for the few days of its run, I can't say who will be in your audience, except that it certainly won't be your parents because nine out of ten of you are from out of town.

How do you expect to pay for this exposure? The girls will find it easier to get some break than the boys, if the girls are not too particular. There are always openings for salesgirls, topless waitresses, and naked Watusi dancers.

Suppose you're lucky, you do get a small part and make a little money. Then you try to live up to your newfound success and start thinking of the next role (which might not be there). You buy, buy, buy cars, clothes, a bigger apartment and go further into debt, because you know you are on your way up. What happens? The next part is a very long time in coming and the bills pile up.

Don't do it. Live on your established income as a waitress, busboy, parking-lot attendant, or clerk, but don't get your hopes up. Nobody is discovered in a soda fountain—it only happens in the dreams of a publicity man.

Many years ago, during the heyday of motion pictures, the actor and actress in Hollywood were viewed with awe by landlords, restaurateurs, clothiers, etc. Realize you've come up the road too late. Take a look in the bankruptcy courts and at the many small-claims cases over past-due bills. The storage houses, row on row of them, are packed with clothing, furniture, automobiles, televisions, and radio sets being held in lieu of payments, confiscated by irate debt holders. Look around at the hundreds of collection agencies in this area. And believe me, most of the time these collectors take action. They go to the expense of hiring lawyers and taking their cases to court and 90 percent of the time they win. You're stuck with original bill, their lawyer fees, and the court costs. Let no one tell you that you can't go to jail for owing money. Perhaps there is no "debtor's prison," but they can lock you up. But they prefer to just strip your assets. Once a judgment is offered against you, the collection agency will deviously attempt to pick up your car (even if you owe money on it to someone else), attach your salary (if you have one), and take your furniture.

They can't get it if you hide it. Move away—get a new address.

But sooner or later, these agencies will find you, your car, your furniture, and your salary. Even if you have hidden all you own, they will find you and then petition the court for a subpoena to demand your appearance in a referee court. You must appear in the referee court, where the referee (judge) will determine your assets. You're under oath now, you'd better not lie. Hide nothing or you're in contempt of court and that means jail and/or a fine.

This, then, is where the debtor prison comes into being. If you neglected to appear in judgment court, it simply means you admit your guilt and a judgment is handed down against you. If you don't appear in referee court, a sheriff shows up at your door and you are escorted to jail in contempt of court. There'll be a fine, possibly jail, and you still have to pay the original judgment, lawyer fees, and court costs.

An interesting situation in a referee court happened recently to a friend of mine. He was served with a subpoena in the wee hours of the morning (when most of them are served). He'd been served before, so he tossed it on the desk and went back to bed. Next morning when he looked at the official document, it proved to be entirely blank except for his name and a judge's signature— all the dotted lines for date and place of appearance, charge, etc. had not been filled in. However, being meticulous with his papers, he filed the subpoena.

Two years later the sheriff appeared at his door and he was hustled off to county jail. But because he was able to produce the blank document, the case was dismissed. He was able to sue the original holder of the debt, the collection agency, and their attorneys, the process server, and the city for false arrest. Needless to say, he won. The collection agency is out of business and the judge who had signed the blank document was dismissed.

Why must you, the potential entrant into the world of entertainment, be confronted with this horrible subject that none of your teachers or correspondence courses ever brought to your attention? It could be they'd rather not mention the dark side of your chosen profession. Would you pay twenty-five dollars an hour for acting lessons, if your teacher told you anything except the glamour and the fabulous rewards?

First of all, what are you really starting out with? Most of you reading these chapters are either in the later years of grade school or teenagers in high school. To you who are really interested, I urge you to find a good drama teacher. They are so few and far between and you'll have to search hard and long. I must go back to the words of the immortal George Bernard Shaw: "Those who can, do. Those who can't, teach." Most high school and college drama teachers do little or no harm because they are not trying to make actors and actresses out of you. It's those who actually think they are *teaching* you to act, who actually believe it themselves, who are the most dangerous. Most are little more than disappointed bit players, and I challenge their right to be dramatic arts teachers if they have not been able to make the grade on the stage, or the screen, themselves. And with lessons from the likes of these so-called teachers, you get credits toward being a doctor and/or a bachelor of dramatic arts (which means only that you can teach in their stead when you've completed their course). Don't think some producer is going to rush out and make you a star simply because you have a sheepskin which says you have completed a course.

Let each of them challenge me. I accept! I have made many films, yet *I* do not teach. I wonder why the schools and colleges hire these never-have-beens. Because they are well versed in the old—and I emphasize *old*—classics? Perhaps. Nevertheless, they continue to teach you how to be professional actors and actresses and they can outtalk anyone on the subject of how the *professionals* do it all wrong—the more successful the actor, financially or critically, the sharper the criticism. I have yet to hear any drama coach tell students the horror or oblivion that is bound to befall them in one way or another.

Don't hurry. Oblivion will be there eventually. The roses of success smell so sweet, but thorns are truly painful, which leads me back to my tirade about the professional drama teacher. Many of them can really help you, in the basics of diction, word placement, dress, poise, and posture. Don't count on walking out of their classes with your diploma and being immediately hired by even the sleaziest of producers. (An afterthought: drama teachers are forever reluctant to let you end the classes. If they do, it would cut into their established income—horror upon horrors.)

The fragrance of the roses has wafted to you from all directions, mostly from a bunch of smelly characters. The thorns will become even more prevalent as the flowers wither and the perfume disintegrates into thin air. The thorns of the real entertainment world, where all the filth has been purposely perfumed, will be ever present as you try to make your way in the business.

There are thorns in the basics of living and eating in Hollywood for the struggling actor. I don't actually know how to get along in Hollywood without some kind of money. But I *can* advise you this far.

Every single city or town in the greater Los Angeles area is flooded, day by day—and I mean every day—with throwaway papers. The papers give the sale prices on items in the markets. Watch for the sales. Pennies will become important, but be sure you don't spend more on gas for your car or bus fare than you'd be saving at the market. The best bet is the market within walking distance and almost anywhere you'll live in the Hollywood area, you'll be within walking distance of a large supermarket.

I have a friend who will drive twenty miles to save six cents on a single can of beans. This is no exaggeration. No one can tell him he is spending thirty-nine cents on gas alone to save six cents on a can of beans, let alone the time he spends, and the wear and tear on his car.

The is the second most important factor to life in Tinsel Town is where to live. Choose wisely, in Hollywood itself the rents are fantastic. Your best bets are in the outlying areas. For instance, in Hollywood a bachelor apartment with a hot plate and bath down the hall can go for fifteen dollars a week.

But then there is always Griffith Park, just off Los Feliz Boulevard between Hollywood and Glendale. The park gates close at 10:00 PM but who will know if you slip in under the fence and sleep on a park bench? Have several blankets, however. It gets cold at night. But it won't cost you a dime if you're not caught!

One guy got away with it for years; he looked like the prototype of all hermits and lived on grass and wild berries. He made the headlines when he was finally found. It hadn't cost him a dime to live for years. Last I heard they were taking him to the rubber room at the happy farm. However, we must give him some credit: *He did live in the Hollywood area without money.*

None of you will ever be satisfied with a small room, at least not for long. All of you, in the beginning, will want prestige addresses and a swimming pool is most desirable. You'll pay for it, too. Once I had an apartment at a prestige address directly across the street from the gates of Warner Brothers—a hundred-and-fifty dollars a month for a two-burner stove, a refrigerator that could hold one ice cube tray and four TV dinners, a front room with beat-up furniture, a small bedroom, and a bathroom that I entered sideways. But I had my prestige address and it had one of the most beautiful swimming pools in the world, set into a U-shaped patio.

When I had business people to entertain, I was the big shot with my pool and my cocktails and my luncheons on the patio. I just had to make sure that nobody ever went up to my apartment. Almost everybody who visited me would need to use the telephone, so I had an extra-long cord that extended from my apartment, over the balcony, and down to the pool. The cord took care of that situation. Did it ever—one month my bill totaled six-hundred dollars.

And the third basic to life in Hollywood: transportation. Of course, there is the taxicab. Expensive and certainly not practical on your budget unless you are the driver. (Many an actor does a taxi-driving stint—I did once upon a time.)

Then the bus. Economical, in a way, and they do get you within a certain proximity of your destination, that is after you've waited on some street corner for the bus that is always late or early. Buses are so few and far between, you wait and you wait with your makeup wilting and your hair coming down and your dress creasing. Make sure to leave early and you *might* make your appointment nearly on time, but with no guarantee of how you'll look when you finally arrive.

In Los Angeles, as nowhere else in the world, you must have an automobile! As the commercials on any station anytime of the day or night on television or radio in the Los Angeles area proclaim—

including Bell, Long Beach, Downey to the south, and the San Fernando Valley to the north—there are more than enough new and used car lots to serve you. The new cars, you can't afford. The used, well, if you can afford anything at all, this is all you can afford at first. If they claim "no down payment," don't you believe it!

The first automobile I purchased in Hollywood was a 1934 Chevy—and I don't mean I bought it in 1934. I was shoved into it in 1951. It lasted from Universal City to the first lamppost on Ventura Boulevard, a distance of perhaps half a mile. Even then, I got off lightly; some barely make it off the car lot. Nothing you can do about it either. Ninety percent of the time, these places have small signs, in hard-to-read areas that bear the legend: "No Guarantee—All Sales Final."

There might be a way to live in Hollywood without money for a time, and mark my words very clearly—only for a time.

The credit card is, of course, the easiest way. Even the lowliest restaurant has some form of credit system. But then again, the first of the month comes around every month. At least you can figure you've had a thirty-day leeway without cash and if you're lucky, or a fast talker, or a pretty girl, you might extend your cashless days to sixty, ninety, maybe even to a hundred-and-twenty. However, the day for payment must come sooner or later.

Credit, however, is extremely important. No working actor or actress works every day of the year, and few work enough to get through the lean days from paycheck to paycheck with cash in their wallets or purses. This is a time your credit will be your one and only lifesaver.

In the beginning, never pay anything in cash if you can get credit. This way you establish your credit rating, and that rating remains constant and good just as long as you pay your bills when they come due.

But I paid for the extras, and you will, too, in the beginning. How to live in Hollywood without money? Outside of Griffith Park, it's impossible!

CHAPTER SEVEN

Sex—Hollywood and You

What makes an actor or actress? I can't define the magic of acting with any facts or logic. I do know, as do most of you, that if something happens on the screen that I like, then I like it, if it's an actor or actress, then I like him or her. (I liked the television series *The Bell Brothers* starring the Bell Brothers, but it seemed few others liked it—the ratings shooed them off the air. Does that make them any less talented as actors? I wouldn't think so, their nightclub dates are at an all-time high.)

I can tell you that very few people ever get their first break in Hollywood, New York, or anywhere else in the world, without being chased around a desk or two—or three or four—by some grubby-handed producers. That goes not only for the girls, but also for the boys. I don't mean by women producers, there are very few women producers.

Sex! It becomes all important. Sex! It becomes more important than any possible talent.

Hard? Sure it's hard, but this is a hard business. If you're not a very good-looking girl or boy, you've got less chance than a snowball in hell of even getting started.

Look in your own mirror, you can tell. Have you ever seen an ugly duckling as a young lead? It just doesn't happen. Look in your own mirror before you even think about listening to your voice on a tape recorder.

Are you presentable? This goes for the boys as well as the girls.

Character people with talent don't need to take a good hard look in the mirror. They always have a better chance—we need new supporting people. The older character people of the entertainment world are passing into eternity, faster than we'd like them to go. This past year we lost Herbert Marshall, Frank Yaconnelli, Addison Richards, Percy Kilbride, and Peter Lorre. Unfortunately, Addison Richards died the same day as Peter Lorre, so Addison was lost to the back pages while Lorre commanded front-page headlines.

But back to you, the newcomer. As I said before, there are a lot of desks you are going to be chased around. Come from wherever you may, from Little Town USA to Big City USA, or anywhere in the world, but be sure to bring your tennis shoes because it will be easier to catch you if you have on high heels.

Perhaps it'd be easier on you to give in first and think about it later.

"To give in, or not to give in" that is the question. Supposing you do, and don't get the part you've been promised—you're labeled. Suppose you do get the part and can't handle it—what kind of chippie does that make you?

Being in the entertainment industry is very much like being in a dark closet. Sometimes a door opens and the light shines in, brightening your area for a time, but in nearly all cases only for a short time. In some cases, the door opens more often, and in a very few cases, the door opens and remains open. Most of the time, the door is closed as quickly as it opened. You search the darkness for even a glimmer of light.

Then you're confronted by an old roué who hasn't made a film since the early 1930s, but still calls himself a producer. I suppose he does have a right: he did make a few cheap, badly staged musicals for 20th Century way back when!

He'll take you girls to his plush office on Sunset Strip. He keeps the office for two reasons: a tax deduction and meeting young girls when he's in town. He likes them young—not always the age of consent either. He's not one to throw the small ones back. He has a hell of a lot of photographs of himself and great stars of the past and present, all over his walls. He'll tell you how much the stars love him, how instrumental he was in getting them started in pictures. You're so awed at his performance, and you forget to figure his age against the ages of those he is supposed to have discovered. He must have been fifteen years old when Wallace Beery and Marie Dressler began their careers.

But there you are; the cloak of darkness has lifted for a moment. You're wearing your beautiful white angora sweater that makes you look so soft and cuddly. He can't keep his eyes off you and wishes from the outset that he didn't have to go through all the preliminaries. He wants his fingers digging into that soft fur.

Here you are actually in the office of this famed personality. You're in his clutches for the time being, but it won't last long. He'll give you his apartment pitch—or perhaps he has a "casting couch" right there in his office. You give in, or you don't give in—either way, it's all over in a few minutes. You're slipping the soft angora sweater over your head, and you're back in the dark again, looking for another way out. Looking for the next beam of light. Looking for the next glimmer or flicker of hope.

In this scenario, this particular producer has delivered you graciously into his office and given you the look-what-I-have-done-for-others act. He's sized you and your angora sweater up with his greedy, ever-prying eyes. Now he opens the right-hand drawer of his desk, pulls out a bottle of expensive perfume, drenches his hands with it, then advances upon you with hands outstretched. "Now we can talk, my dear."

At least with this character you'll leave the office with a sweet-smelling angora sweater. Fix your lipstick. This guy has thin lips, the better to smear you with, my dear.

In the case of another producer, your choice is an easy one. He has an office. You become offended, tell him so, and tell him that you'll scream. You get safe conduct out of the office. He can't afford a scream, because people all over the building will hear you. There is another, more nefarious Sunset Strip producer. This one has never made a film in his life, as a producer, or an actor, or a writer, or anything else. But he does have photographs all over his office of him shaking hands, or hugging, well-known personalities. The only problem is that the pictures are really of his twin brother, who is a tremendous—but not famous—terror. This so-called producer has been living on his brother's talents for years. The sheriff closes him down every few months, and the district attorney has put him in prison a few times. Each and every time he is released, his office opens again for the new and unsuspecting. His newspaper ads never change over the years: "Actors/Actresses Wanted for Radio/Movies/Television. No Experience Necessary."

I met this freak in 1949 when I first came to Hollywood and responded to his ad. My experience was fairly limited. I had answered a previous ad for a writer in the *Los Angeles Times*. You must realize in 1948, I was a rank beginner who could criticize everyone else's work but couldn't sell any of my own. This was the first ad I'd ever answered in my life. I'd been in the Hollywood area since 1947, living with a very wonderful ex-Marine family. Except for a brief stint at the Broadway Department Store one Christmas, I hadn't had a job and was worried about straining their hospitality.

This first ad turned out to be for Bell International Theater Workshop. Bell International Studio was a building on Sunset Boulevard, which has since become a fence over the Hollywood Freeway. A strange thing about the ad—it was legitimate. The owner wanted a writer for the professional screen tests they specialized in producing. I can't remember the old man's name, but I wish I could, so I could give him credit here. He was a giant of a man in the industry, but I'm sure he's long gone, into eternity or obscurity— I don't know. I wish he were still around, he could have been important to those of you coming up with his personality, force, dedication. He charged six-hundred dollars for a three-minute screen test on 16mm color film. He was as likely to advance his own money to young people he believed in as he was to accept a check.

Despite my lack of professional experience, he hired me as a writer. I sold myself by showing him a short story called "Final Curtain," (later filmed for television, starring C. J. Moore).

My employment lasted over a year, and during that time, I met and became lifelong friends with Walter Kohner of the famed Paul Kohner agency and also met the greatest cameraman of all time to my mind: Ray Flin. (His latest series is *McHale's Navy*.) But as all good things must end, the drama studio closed and I was looking for work again.

"Actors/Actresses Wanted for Radio/Movies/Television. No Experience Necessary." That ad. I answered that ad. I arrived sometime around nine o'clock in the morning. I met the producer, read for him, and was cast in his new radio show, which he assured me "will go to television when television comes in." (And it was coming in fast in those days.)

"Report here tomorrow morning at seven to begin rehearsals." I'll remember his dramatic pause and his next line all the years of my life. "You do have a union card?"

"What union?"

"AFRA." His tone became pointed. "American Federation of Radio Artists."

"No!"

His blue eyes looked up to me. "We'll fix that for you. The initiation fee is two-hundred-and-fifty dollars." Pause. He was coy. "You can arrange that?"

I was in my glory. I was to be a radio star in a series. I'd done several radio shows before, as an amateur but to be a *regular*—sure I had the two-fifty. He waved me away.

"Leave the money with my secretary in the outer office."

I did just that . . . left my money with her.

I was there at 7 AM the next morning. I sat on the curb until 7 PM. That's a long time. About 7:30, the producer came in. He claimed not to remember me—he had never seen me before. I argued.

"But here's my receipt for the two-hundred-and-fifty dollars I paid you yesterday for my union card."

"That's not my signature!"

"It's your secretary's."

He pointed to a new girl behind the secretary's desk. "That's my secretary, and that's certainly not her name. I can't be responsible for any other."

He'd hired this one the night before. And I was out two-hundred-and-fifty dollars.

I've been slowly vindicated, however, over the years as I've read in the newspapers that this particular man has received a year here and a year there in prison for his girlie activities. Not once has he been convicted for bilking young people the way he did me. His convictions are always for bothering young girls—he is rarely troubled by their legal ages.

His scam runs something like this. The producer has a radio booth, ostensibly so that he can hear your voice recorded under radiolike quality. He asks you to enter that booth and record for him. Why would you deny him this? He's the producer, after all, hasn't he got the pictures on the wall to prove it? The radio booth is soundproof. You can scream your head off as he pulls the angora sweater over your head, but no one can hear you. He'll see that you take plenty of time after it's over and his lust is satisfied to get properly dressed again. He won't let you leave the office looking ragged. It might reflect on him.

As a bonus, your screams, squeals, pleadings, and his panting could be recorded. I'm sure he'll sell you a copy of the tape if you'd like it. He's made quite a business out of that kind of thing, too.

Sour grapes for my lost two hundred and fifty? No. I make pictures. I don't have to prey, like a vulture, on the beginner. You must remember that I was also a beginner. And I met the same snakes out for my money as those who came up before me, as you will meet, and as those who come up after you will meet. These leeches out for the bucks your dad gave you outlive the innocent and lie in wait for the next batch of newcomers.

You! It's easy to see why. They have one pitch. They stick to it and, in general, get a great deal of sex along with the cash. Why put in any hard work that could advance them to a heart attack? They invented the pitch thirty or more years ago, it was a success for them, so they stay with it. Two-hundred-fifty dollars is a pretty fair day's wages for a half an hour's talk with some kid. How many others do you think answered the ad the same day I did? It doesn't take much ingenuity to hire a new secretary every night, does it?

So, am I for answering ads or against it? Neither! Just take care of yourself, that's all. Many of the advertisers are respectable, some are not. Some are just so sad, some just a come-on or an invitation to sex.

Recently I met a young lady who had finished just one film. She had come from Mississippi and was heading back the way she had come as quickly as Trailways could get her there. She was disillusioned beyond consolation. She had landed in Hollywood with a few dollars, which were soon gone. One advantage she did have was her youth (she was eighteen) and her beautiful face and figure. A well-known actor happened upon her in a bar, took her home with him, and promised her the world. After some times spent under the sheets in his apartment, he did finally get her a bit part. She was to run through a desolate park trail in her panties and brassiere, with a rapist chasing her. In the scene, she finds a telephone booth but has no coin to make it work, so the rapist catches and murders her. The location scene went well, but the telephone booth segment had to be filmed on stage to get the sound recorded. The director had the girl on call at 5 AM for tedious hours of makeup everyday day in and day out. But he just couldn't get to her scene. The more important actors, the ones costing him the most money, took precedent. Day after day, this kid from Mississippi got up at 4 AM to be on the set and in makeup at 5 AM, and in hairdressing by 6 AM. Then she would languish until all hours of the night. Finally, at a lunch break one day, she was fed up. Right in the middle of the commissary, she stood up, looked the director straight in his eye, and shouted, "I screwed an actor to get into this business. Who in hell do I screw to get out of it?"

Her final sequence was filmed immediately after lunch. She used the money to return to Mississippi a little heavier than when she'd arrived in Hollywood. There was a child in her abdomen, and she knew not who the father was.

Don't think this can't happen to you. It has happen to many who have come up this trail to Tinsel Town believing it couldn't possibly happen to them. My friend Lieutenant Karl Johnson (son of the famous Swedish Angel and great horror film actor) of the San Fernando Police Department can relate stories of sex and how sex leads to dope and how dope leads to smut films that can not only degrade your very being, but end your career forever as the coffin lid fits over your head in Forest Lawn cemetery.

There is a time for living and a time for dying. Most of you who read this have just experienced your first bout with sex. The boy next door . . . the high school cheerleader . . . a friend around the corner . . . the delivery boy . . . the school chippie. You think you can handle anything that comes along. Believe me, you can't. There are too many who have been up the road ahead of you who have learned ways, means, and devices that could stand you on your head—and I've heard of it being done *while* standing on your head also.

The movie industry is not all about screenplays or standing in front of cameras. Moviemaking is, to say the least, a dangerous business.

For every legitimate producer, there are dozens of phonies! Then add to that the corrupt actors, writers, and agents. You're fighting a thousand to one chance of losing every cent you have or can muster and your virginity to boot, without ever seeing the inside of a studio.

You'll probably become acquainted with an actor long before you ever meet a producer or director. There are places, easily found in Tinsel Town, where actors—mostly bit players—hang out. And what line you'll hear from him until you take your angora sweater off in his room (few can afford apartments). Then, after it's all over you'll hear, "Get lost, honey." He's already on the make for someone else.

You must realize you are only one of many to him. There's always another new one, wearing a different sweater, coming up the road directly behind you. Who are you? Just another sex venture who has fed his ego for the moment.

Actually, I dislike writing about my town in this way. But I'm not really writing about the town or those who make the films. I'm trying to paint a factual picture of what happens to you, the newcomer, the inexperienced kid who is preyed upon by every sharpie who sees you.

Of course there are the truly big producers and directors who do who act out of line at times, and I doubt very much if any of them *wouldn't* take your angora sweater off given the chance. Even legitimate producers and directors are human. But to find the difference between the phony and the real is tough. I could list the distinctions here for page after page, and name after name, office after office, but then I'd have lawsuit after lawsuit. So I must content myself with this warning to enlighten you: they are here, both legitimate and illegitimate.

It's up to you as to how you want to play the game. Take your chances standing up or on your back.

"It's not the dark I fear—it's the things that move around in it."

CHAPTER EIGHT

Hate

I've spent many hours pondering those actors who hate Hollywood. There has been an influx of people who somehow manage to get into *our* guilds and *our* unions, by hook or by crook, yet trumpet their disdain for our fair city.

Not many professions are refuges for people who loath the very business that provides their livelihood. And though few make it into movies even briefly, a good percentage of those who succeed look down on the Hollywood industry. Truthfully they are, in most cases, extremely bad actors or actresses in the first place, and they always focus on the negative aspects of whatever they chose.

The New York Stage, they shout! That's the only place for an actor or actress! That's the only place to really act. They shout at the top of their lungs to all who will listen, and their shouting is so loud that those of us who don't care to listen have our hearing devices infiltrated anyway. We cannot ignore them.

Yet I don't even care to ignore them—I want to know these "haters." I want to know who they are with their big mouths and their small ideologies, so I won't have to hire them for my films. You'd be surprised as to how many other directors and producers feel as I do. Then again, since most of you are beginners, you probably didn't realize these people exist. You never read about such things in your fan magazines, but Hollywood has its own special kind of nut.

If you hate a job—no matter what type or what field—how can you make a success of it? Your negative thoughts destroy anything good you are trying to accomplish. How can your employer be expected to keep you on? Why should a film producer hire actors who hate the very films that support them, at the expense of those of you on the unemployment line?

Of course, there are many more actors and actresses (past, present, and future) than there are parts in film and television. But compare how many parts open every day in many films (both movie and television) to the number of parts available in live theater. Every year or two, I assure you, rather than every day as in film. I contend that these loudmouth haters of films put in the opposite situation—on the New York stage—would hate the stage and pine for Hollywood.

I don't understand these people. I've loved films since I was an usher collecting throwaway stills from the ash cans behind the theater. Even as a small child I was hooked, back in the time when my dad bought an old hand-cranked Keystone movie projector and a few comedies. I've worked really hard at what I love—I even raised the money for my first film. Actually, I don't hate any form of entertainment because each has its place in the pantheon. And I have worked professionally in all forms: stage, screen, radio, television, nightclubs, even carnivals and circuses. How could I hate any aspect of the entertainment world I've been connected to all my life?

Entertaining the public is a privilege and not a right. Anyone with the love for and the ability to entertain others is fortunate to make a living at it and should fall on his or her knees raising eyes to God to thank the heavens for that privilege.

The beginner should realize this before undertaking any career.

An actor or actress—a real one—is an actor or actress, no matter what the medium. You must learn early that a really good actor or actress is going to have to appear in each of the mediums sooner or later, including a few I've not listed.

I can tell you about the unexpected career turn of the well-known film actor and my friend, the late Bela "Dracula" Lugosi. Mr. Lugosi was famous because of his cinematic appearances, but unbeknownst to all except his most ardent fans and family he was also a great stage personality. Certainly thousands, perhaps millions, of fans would have been neglected had he confined his brilliance to the screen. Of course, he created Dracula on stage long before Universal pictures made it into a film in 1938. And he was a giant of a personality on radio. I can attest to this—I've heard the fantastic tale of his life story over nationwide hook-up.

But Bela Lugosi! I never heard Bela say he hated movies. As with all great actors, he did become despondent at times about his career when films were not coming as regularly as he would have liked. By 1953, the baby art called television was a baby no longer, but a skeleton filling out toward the giant it was to become.

And a giant needs much to eat! In the case of the television giant's diet . . . film! Film and more film! Motion pictures became its steady diet. Film and still more film. Eventually Universal Pictures released Bela's backlog of movies. *White Zombie* was first to hit the television screen on KHJ-TV in Los Angeles, California, with a new personality, Vampira, presiding as host (a very lovely blonde young lady named Maila Nurmi who in later years starred in my *Plan 9 from Outer Space*). And with a great fanfare of advertising in local newspapers, KTLA, also of Los Angeles, presented the great—the original—*Dracula.*

New generations were enjoying the master of horror at work for the first time. Previous generations were enthralled to see this great man again. But still, there were no television stations or television filmmakers clamoring for his services.

Bela, then seventy-one years of age, became even more despondent than before. He seemed ready to give up, to quit, to finish the whole business. He was ill—more ill than any of us who knew him realized. But as physically ill as he was and as outwardly ready to quit, his mind was alert and his inner self would never let him really give up.

One afternoon I was lounging in his apartment, discussing the latest world problems he'd been reading in the newspaper. (Bela did most of the talking as he certainly was more up on world affairs than I probably ever will be.) Suddenly, he let his pen fall to the floor near the arm of his giant leather reclining chair. He leaned his head back with closed eyes. For a long moment he was silent. Then, he began to talk in that glorious, distinct, Hungarian voice which many have tried to imitate but have failed.

"Eddie," he started, with his eyes still closed. "I have just read an article which disturbs me very much."

"What's that, Bela?" I was bewildered at his sudden change in attitude. There was a tremendous hurt in his voice.

"Some kids wrote to the television station that played *Dracula* last week. They wondered if Bela Lugosi is still alive." He opened his eyes and looked directly at me before he spoke again. "These kids! They see my old movies. You know, Eddie, the kids are not dumb today like many would like us to believe. They know the pictures on television are old movies. They can add! They know the pictures are not new. No wonder the kids ask if I am alive—or dead."

"What do you think we can do about it, Bela?" It was all I could think of to say.

"Me? What do I think? You are the writer! You are the promoter! What are you going to do about it?"

For days this became the most important question in my life. What was the right way to reintroduce Bela to the public?

But it became apparent to me that whatever was to be done must be accomplished with Bela in direct physical contact with his audience. But a play at this stage of his life would have been too trying, so there was only one way. Personal appearances! The time and the situation had to be just right.

When I broached the subject of personal appearances with Bela in early December 1953, he was filled with enthusiasm. I felt I was seeing his face glow with true happiness for the first time in many months.

"A personal appearance!" He beamed as he sat on the floor in front of his gigantic oil painting. "Just what I want." His exuberance was mounting. Then his voice suddenly became a monotone without losing its exactness, he said, "Where do we start?"

Another question of great magnitude: "Just where in hell do we start?"

I'd had some experience with a few motion picture stars in stage appearances, but each had a vaudeville act of one kind or another which an audience could readily accept. Bela had no act in the vaudeville sense of the word. He didn't sing. He didn't dance. He didn't tell family stories. He didn't play a musical instrument or do magic tricks.

This was an excellent idea to bring Bela before his dearly loved public, but the exact venue kept eluding me.

At the time, I was presenting a western stage show, which had shown some minor success at motion picture theaters throughout the area, owned by Mr. Albert Stetson. It was then an inspiration hit me.

I mentioned to Mr. Stetson that Bela Lugosi had decided to go on tour and meet his public in person.

"What kind of an act does he have?"

There was the horrifying question again.

"None."

What else could I have said?

Mr. Stetson's office was on a spacious, deeply carpeted, fashionably decorated mezzanine. His office was comparably small, but well decorated: carpeted, furnished, and cluttered with press books, newspaper clippings, motion picture ad sheets, and all that goes with his end of the business. Mr. Stetson, a trim, extremely well-dressed, bespectacled man wearing a bow tie, leaned forward across his desk. For a long moment it was apparent he was in deep thought. The he looked at me seriously.

He had an idea. And Mr. Stetson was ready to back up his idea with his own cold hard cash.

That plan went into its final stage—Bela Lugosi's personal appearance on the stage of Mr. Stetson's San Bernardino, California theater on the night of December 31, 1953. New Year's Eve.

Being the trooper he was, Bela made several trips from Hollywood to San Bernardino in the days before his appearance. He held press conferences, gave interviews over radio stations, and presided toastmaster at ladies clubs, men's organizations, and cocktail parties—all to boost ticket sales and audience attendance.

Bela prized a photograph taken during this period. It was taken as he presented ticket to "admit one" to Mayor Blair, then mayor of San Bernardino. Bela felt the man was doing an excellent job for a worthwhile community. Bela had always been interested in communities across the world as well as the government in Washington itself. Never did he shy away from voicing his own opinions.

It was cold! Very cold! No rain was falling but a wet mist sat over the entire sixty-old miles from Los Angeles to San Bernardino as Bela, his lovely assistant Miss Dolores Fuller (a motion picture actress in her own right), and myself made the journey to Mr. Stetson's theater for the night's entertainment. Mr. Stetson arranged comfortable suites at a leading hotel for both Bela and Miss Dolores before show time, but what Mr. Stetson had not mentioned was that there was to be little rest for either of them.

There was immediately another radio interview. More publicity photographs were again taken at the theater and then a final cocktail party for the press. It was designed along the lines of a Hollywood premiere but, thinking back, it grew into a much more heartwarming, rewarding experience.

The cocktail party progressed. Bela, who had always enjoyed his scotch and room temperature beer, refrained from even a cordial. But I could see he was getting extremely tired and nervous. It was six PM, and it was beginning to look as though the cocktail hour would go straight through the dinner hour and possibly beyond.

I found Mr. Stetson and his charming wife getting a breath of fresh air outside on the hotel patio. I admired Mrs. Stetson's green taffeta dress and exchanged a few pleasantries with her, then turned to Mr. Stetson. I wasn't harsh in my demands, but I was definite.

"If Bela is going to appear on your stage at ten nineteen, I think we'd better end this gathering now. He's answered hundreds of questions about *Dracula* and explained why he refused the part of the Frankenstein monster at least anther hundred times. He's not as young as Miss Fuller, you know."

Mr. Stetson's face changed noticeably. "It is getting a bit too much, isn't it?"

He went back into the room and made his short speech of dismissal to the assembly. A few minutes later, I was taking my friend Bela to his hotel suite. A fifth of scotch, a fifth of bourbon, and several bottles of room temperature beer had been provided for us on a portable bar.

I went immediately to the bar and poured myself a large whiskey, which I drank straight.

"Ready for one, Bela?"

He had not had a drink of anything stronger than coffee throughout the evening. "Not tonight, my friend. Is my full dress suit ready?"

"The bellboy is having it pressed. He'll have it here before show time."

"I'm becoming very nervous!"

"Haven't you ever been nervous before?"

"Every time I go before an audience . . . I want a drink!"

"It's right there." I pointed to the bar.

"I want a drink, Eddie. But not tonight. Not just now." He stretched his full length on the bed. Suddenly he snapped up again. "My cape is not being pressed."

"Just being steamed as you directed."

"Good." He went down again and was silent while I poured another whiskey. "Eddie . . . do you think they will like me tonight?"

"They'll love you, Bela."

"Do you think I am doing enough for my public?"

"Mr. Stetson does and he's the one paying the bills."

He became more insistent. "But what do you think?"

"Let's put it this way, Bela. You need to meet the public. It's important to your career. I'm also sure the public wants to meet you. You don't sing. You don't dance. Let's just say, the idea is sound. And here we have a springboard to see what happens. As you said earlier, we have to start somewhere."

He thought a moment, then looked directly at me again. "So I am sandwiched between five features—a gross of cartoons and a hundred-dollar bank night drawing. How are we to find out if it is me they come to see?"

What could I say? There really were five features, several cartoons, and a hundred-dollar bank night drawing. I repeated, "We have to start somewhere."

"I know, Eddie—I know." His eyes were closed, but it was apparent he was becoming more restless and more uncomfortable. "Miss Fuller is a lovely girl. She'll be an asset. Do you have a cigar?"

"You know I never smoke cigars, Bela, look in your pocket!"

"Oh, yes." He took out one of the extremely long cigars Mr. Stetson had presented to him, tipped off the end, and lighted it, before he spoke again. "I want to sleep for a while, after I take my medicine."

"Okay, Bela. I'll see you at nine-thirty."

He became very silent, letting tremendous clouds of gray cigar smoke drift up around his head. Those hypnotic eyes looked toward the green-gray ceiling.

I left the room at that point and paused long enough to light a cigarette. I think I heard a key turn in the lock. Bela, for the moment, demanded solitude even from his friends.

At nine PM, a reissue film starring Jon Hall entitled *Arabian Nights* was presented. The theater housed so few people you could shoot a canon off down the aisles without hitting a living soul.

Mr. Stetson was pacing the floor in his office. I was slumped in a chair just off the main lobby below the mezzanine. I wasn't happy about the attendance.

Then it happened! A newspaper man, slightly tipsy from the cocktail party given in Bela's honor, and his white-satin clothed wife, came into the theater with purchased tickets. He shouted to the doorman, "Where's Mr. Wood?"

Hearing this, I went to the man and his wife. "You want me?"

He stuck out his hand. "This better be you!" He scowled. "The show, I mean." Then he laughed. "I've got the power of the press behind me, you know."

That was all he said, then he and his wife moved on into the darkness of the theater. Possibly he was the Pied Piper of Hamelin, or it was mere coincidence. But something tremendous began to happen. The dispenser's bell began to ring as if by an incessant door-to-door salesman.

Mr. Stetson came out of his office. He looked down toward his ticket booth. The line outside was forming. I caught the broad grin on his features. He had made it. The girl in his ticket booth was spinning out tickets as fast as she could press the automatic buttons.

Then a sadness crossed his features. Mr. Stetson returned to his office. He closed the door. It was apparent that at that moment Mr. Stetson realized he had delivered the audience, but would the public get what they were paying for.

I was not able to meet Bela at nine-thirty. That duty fell to Miss Fuller and Mrs. Stetson. Fifteen minutes before Bela was to appear on stage, the police and fire departments arrived. The streets were clogged with traffic and surrounding parking lots were filled with cars. The theater box office displayed Standing Room Only signs. Yet the line continued to lengthen. The fire department was forced to clear the aisles inside the theater. The police department was forced to make a path on E Street to permit traffic to pass, and they were forced also to keep disappointed fans from tearing the theater front apart.

Arabian Nights ended at 10:10. A cartoon entitled *Runaway Mouse* ended at 10:19. The house lights went up.

The curtain came down!

Bela was outside getting out of the limousine.

Even his two lovely companions, Miss Fuller and Mrs. Stetson, had to step aside as people on the ticket line rushed to Bela for his autograph.

I could tell by the glow on Bela's face that he understood, even before a fireman explained, there would be no more people allowed inside the theater. The crowd grew larger and larger. Traffic became even more congested, and the problems of logistics increased. Teenagers screamed as their elders wanted tickets. The problem became more imperative. A rerun movie and a gross of cartoons hadn't attracted people from parties on New Year's Eve. It was *the* great Lugosi who had come out of hiding after all those years.

On the inside, the fire department diligently fought to keep the aisles open—there were already too many people in the theater.

Two minutes of eleven.

As all things must, the moment arrived. The lights came on. A green-tinted spotlight framed itself against the curtain. The great man walked on stage in full dress suit with the Dracula cape flowing behind him. He looked to his audience.

Then he spoke.

"My dear friends." The tears of joy were beginning to fill the sensitive eyes that had frightened millions. "I greet you here tonight on a new, great, New Year. May the coming year bring the joy and success deserved. I wish, with all my heart, that I might meet each of you on the mezzanine in a few minutes where I might personally shake your hand and say . . . God bless you."

The great man retraced his steps. Tinted green lights died quickly and were replaced by yellow footlights.

An almost deafening silence prevailed. A silence that became unbearably uncomfortable to me.

Mr. Stetson and I were standing at the back of the theater. We were listening to the silence. There was no sound of breathing. Not a cough or sigh. I felt Mr. Stetson's eyes turning toward me. I couldn't look at him.

He had designed the idea. But I had accepted it and I had written the three-minute speech. But Bela had designed his own speech—less than a minute. Bela had spoken from his heart and mind and decided how he wanted to reach to the public.

For a long, long, long moment, dimmed yellow lights played against a dark velvet curtain. Then tear-filled crowds began to applaud. The applause became a clamor. Mr. Stetson's face was beaming. His idea had not only paid off at the box office, but it had won the hearts of the audience. He was beaming. So was I.

After his speech, Bela went to the mezzanine, where he and Miss Fuller gave autographed photographs to the hundreds of fans who mobbed them. Several minutes after Bela's exit and the fantastic applause, the newspaper man, no longer tipsy, found me in the lobby. "This is the first New Year's Eve I've ever spent in the theater. My wife demanded it. I resented it." Then he smiled broadly. "It's been a rewarding experience."

The man and his misses left before I could express our thanks.

Only the letter from Mr. Stetson can successfully close this meaningful episode in Bela Lugosi's life, although there were a great many left.

"When the manager of a motion picture theater fills all his seats, he feels just wonderful. And I certainly do just feel that way tonight. Tonight every seat was filled. And we had nearly two-hundred people waiting.

Our capacity is 1,250 seats. Our ticket sales at eleven PM, for tonight's show, totaled 1,417. What a great satisfaction this must be to Mr. Bela Lugosi. And how our audience loved him. And what a grand trouper he is. The smiles on their faces when they realized they were really, truly, standing in front of the great Dracula just made your heart warm.

"Please convey to Mr. Lugosi my deep, personal appreciation for all that he so generously did to contribute to promoting the personal appearance at our theater.

"Our theater now has newly established records for both attendance and gross business. Tonight was the highest of both since my brother and I took over the theater's operation.

"Mr. Bela Lugosi's personal appearance at the West Coast Theater has truly given our theater a wonderful evening."

—Albert Stetson

Oh, how could Bela ever hate Hollywood.

This episode gave Bela the courage to take on another act so late in his life. In his seventies, he appeared in nightclubs, including the Silver Slipper in Las Vegas. He was willing to tackle a very new role since he was neither a song-and-dance man or a teller of funny stories. When the Herdan-Sherrell Agency informed me that the publicity director of the Silver Slipper, Eddie Fox, thought Lugosi would be a great draw (his films were coming fast and furious on television), I immediately called the grand old man and told him.

"What in hell could I do in a nightclub?"

"Pick up a good check," I said, then I added. "Let me figure out the routine." And I worked with that very funny man of the Silver Slipper Hank Henry to do just that. We designed a nightclub routine, a comedy, for a very serious actor.

This was February of 1954, so very close to the end of Bela's life. His contracted four-week engagement lasted seven weeks. The review said it all:

"By the way, Bela Lugosi has assuredly found himself a new career. . . . This old horror man is such a gentle, lovable guy, the entire Slipper cast to a man can't do enough for him. The Bela Lugosi Review is a show you can see again and again for new experiences every time."

Then there is my friend and partner in many enterprises: Mr. Kenne Duncan, "The Meanest Man in Movies." He has some three or four hundred films to his credit, as well as many plays (there was a time when he was considered a rival to Clark Gable).

Kenne has been a villain to almost every cowboy hero you see in Westerns on film or television. At the end of the picture, he is always outdrawn by the hero—shot down and killed where he stands.

In reality Kenne is one of the best trick shots in the world. While his films show him as the villain who couldn't shoot his way out of a paper bag, his nightclub and carnival acts depict a different story. For this stereotyping, Kenne should hate movies.

His seven-thousand-dollar house car and his eight-thousand-dollar Higgins yacht tell us differently. He is an entertainer who loves to work a variety of parts in a variety of venues. Who can hate the business that loves you and rewards you.

And he has been rewarded: how many cowboy actors have been accepted by the Moulin Rouge in Hollywood? How many embark on world tours? In 1951 Kenne even rode Emperor Hirohito's white horse down Tokyo's main street and he has color newsreel film to prove it. We recently used this footage in a film about Kenne's act.

Every Christmas our boys in the armed services demand Kenne. His latest was with the famed western troupe, the Tex Ritter show. Last year, Kenne spent eleven months touring Spain—keep in mind, Kenne is not a juvenile any longer. How could Kenne hate Hollywood and the films that have made him famous and loved by people all over the world?

Who are these people who hate Hollywood? Perhaps a bunch of communists? They seem to infiltrate everything with their hate campaigns. But if people have been hating Hollywood since movies began, then how could it be a communist-inspired phenomenon? I didn't say it was communist inspired, I said "perhaps." Communism was around when movies began, you just didn't hear about it so much. But there have always those people who shouted their hatred of Hollywood.

Just as there will probably never be any demise of the haters, there will be no demise of Hollywood either. I just sit back in wonder and I ponder.

CHAPTER NINE

Nudie Cuties

A few years ago the nudie film was unheard-of with the exception of a few sleazy movie houses on side streets in a few of the larger towns. Not only was it unheard-of, but it was virtually against the law in most states. Censor boards slapped condemned stickers on these films before they even opened.

Then things began to happen: the box-office receipts were diminishing with each passing month wherever conventional features were shown. Motion picture houses were closing all over the country. Some of the larger studios were closing their doors forever, some studios were being torn down to make room for supermarkets and parking lots. The Hal Roach Studio gave us so many wonderful hours with Laurel and Hardy and the Keystone Cops—today it is a weed-grown vacant lot. The Chaplin lot—an Eagle Lion supermarket. The Monogram studio plot—a set of ghostlike structures.

Television made its grand entrance and the pattern for enter-tainment changed forever. Why should the viewer leave the comfort of his house to pay exorbitant prices in a theater when the same entertainment can be had at home for free?

It was apparent that the producer of movies had to come up with something new, and fast. 3-D didn't make it, either because of the glasses or the subject matter. The wide screens approach helped but it still wasn't enough. The film themselves had to adjust to the scope the wider screens were giving them. The camera was taking in more for the eye to see, so movies could corner the violence market and could capture more than the imagination.

But how long could violence alone hold the public's interest? Mystery stories, little drawing room comedies, and dramas were things of the past. The mysteries of space travel held the public's attention for a time, but the more the fantasy of space became a reality, the more the box-office receipts fell off again.

Far-thinking producers began to defy the ancient outmoded laws of censorship—even pointing to our rights under the Constitution—and presented films of stark reality. These censorship cases pushed the limits before the courts, all the way to the Supreme Court. Censorship itself was censored and controversial films were permitted to go into release. There is very little left which is censurable today. Thus obscenities and naked bodies came into the film world. References to the sex act became depictions with audiences demanding more!

Even the Westerns got into the swing of sex. No longer did the cleanly dressed cowboy kiss his horse and ride off into the sunset to begin another adventure. Instead, he began to wear the dirtiest clothing, kick his horse in the ass, and take the roughest dance hall broad into the hayloft with him.

Once upon a time Dracula and Frankenstein scared us. Now it would seem only violent sex can shock the audience and it seems to be working. The audiences for such films have never been larger. Many of the smaller theaters which had closed their doors ten years ago are opening again and being renovated for pure comfort: new seats, new wide screens, air conditioning. And these are the smaller houses that are not even going to get *Cleopatra*, *Psycho*, or the really big hits.

It is these movie houses which must depend on the smaller films put out by independent producers—films not of the quality of the majors. Most of these films, I must say, may be cleaning up at the box office, but are not cleaning up anyone's mind or morals. These particular films have no purpose beyond titillating with sex and the naked female, of course, and it wouldn't be difficult to determine what kind of person is buying a ticket. There are perverts in all walks of life who can find something in these films. Of course, there are the "sleazy producers" who put out pure, unadulterated crap strictly for this type of demented individual. These films are usually made in some garage with no production cost outside the film itself. The so-called actors and actresses might demand ten dollars for their services!

Sleazy producers are the scourge of all producers of films who are trying to make an entertaining picture. The sleazy producer is by no means in the same category as the independent producer who, for simple economic reasons, must put his picture out on a small budget. The independent does, however, try to put out an entertaining picture on his budget, which does not venture into the obscene. He knows that today's films must have some measure of sex, but he also knows how far he can go for decency's sake. The true independent producer does believe in decency. Because of the possibility of law problems and because he has to live with himself, the indie producer feels that he is a servant of the public and must keep its respect if he is to keep his own.

You must not expect the classic image of Hollywood. One walks the streets of Hollywood today and can hardly tell the boys from the girls: the long hair, the velvet shirts, the Capri pants, and high-heeled boots. Even some of the boys have taken to wearing light pink lipstick while the girls have eliminated that cosmetic. But isn't this, then, show biz? Hollywood is not as the fan magazines attempt to paint. You'd be surprised how many of the boys prefer girl's clothes and the girls who prefer boy's clothes! And I mean big stars, directors, producers, and writers!

Tinsel Town's two main streets, Hollywood Boulevard and Sunset Boulevard have undergone drastic changes. Sunset Boulevard was once the shabbier of the two, but it is now progressing to be one of the foremost modern streets in the world, with tall buildings of black glory granite and shining steel. Hollywood Boulevard, once the Mecca of Hollywood, has become shabby and outmoded.

Ah, our world, as well as my town is changing . . . and it's all because we're growing up. The writer has a greater freedom of expression. Everyone is allowed to celebrate his or her own personality and that personality might not be exactly what you were brought up to believe.

I suppose this chapter really comes down to just that—the existence of the unexpected!

Speaking of the unexpected, you never know what type character you might have to play, should you get the chance. Just how in hell do you expect to play a character if you don't understand him or her, or if you deny his or her existence? You need to come out of your cocoon and realize that reality is the "go-go" of today's film presentations. There is a point of fantasy and point of reality.

You are not going to land a job with one of the major studios—or with an independent—your first time out. But, you could, possibly, land one with a sleazy, and all of his ten dollars. Let's discuss those ten dollars.

Usually the sleazy has no office, just a telephone and perhaps desk space at a garagelike studio where they will shoot the picture. Don't count on the telephone number remaining the same—the bill is very seldom paid so the phone is removed. This is the major reason why the telephone company charges all motion picture companies a large deposit before they can have a phone.

The sleazy doesn't register as a producer, because he doesn't want to be checked on too closely. In addition to the law, every union in town would be on his trail. The whole operation is kept pretty secret. And all but a few of these are considered "tittie" films. There is little or no story line, just one weak excuse after another in incident after incident, so the girls can take their clothes off in front of the camera.

These movies are often made more for the enjoyment of the producer–director than his audience. Certainly the girls who work in them don't enjoy it. The ten bucks won't go far even on a minimum eating budget, but you may remember that ten dollars all your life. Once you see the film you'll want to vomit. And you'll wonder how in the world you could have sunk so low! And mark my words, that film is going to be around a long time after you're gone. The film will be turning up where you least expect it, especially if you make any sort of a name for yourself. Fame lives on fame! The ever-increasing monster. You're only as good as your last picture!

Back to the time you're working on the set of sleaze. Generally you pay for your own lunch, transportation, and you furnish your own wardrobe. Don't let that throw you, the word "wardrobe" may mean a lot to the legitimate producer, but to the sleazy, just about anything you have in your closet will please him. And more than a few of them will be undressed and into *your* dress or sweater and skirt, almost before you've got them off. They just love wearing female attire. (Just as a passing observation, many of your favorite movie actors go in for this fantastic fetish. Horror of a lawsuit keeps me from naming names.)

Another thing to remember is the obscenity laws of the country are not consistent. Certain things you do on film may be legal in one state while a warrant is issued for your arrest in another. Sex is a violent and dangerous business—don't you ever forget it!

For every decent film, there are dozens of these sex films being made every month—and dozens of you will work in them. You will find yourself in them, if you stay in the Hollywood rat race any length of time.

Sooner of later you will meet Mr. Sleazy—probably sooner! He's got a fast line to convince you and an even faster technique to get your clothes off and get you onto his casting couch. Strange as it may seem, a few of these characters will let you just stay on your back, nude, while they try on your clothes. Your panties, warm with the heat of your body, your sweater of an expensive and, usually, a furry nature are hot items to these characters. You could end up doubling, even tripling, your ten-dollar offer if you'll give them the desired articles. However, be prepared to watch as the producer practices weird rituals of self-gratification.

Clothing is only one of these strange fetishes. There are those who like to see the girl tied, or chained to a chair, gagged, while he curses and spews filth at her—always keeping on hand in his trouser pocket. Still another would have you walk over his naked body with your spike-heeled shoes. And these are the tame demands—there are much worse.

All that glitters is not gold! And it would seem that all movies are not the glitter your fan magazines promise.

You might think this is sour grapes—such things couldn't be, such things shouldn't be said of the land where you believed only beauty existed. Get that out of your mind right now! This book is not meant to be an appendix to some fan magazine. When I took on this project, I wanted to reminisce as well as get the point across as to what it's all really like in my Tinsel Town.

You see, you are good business to Hollywood—good business in every facets of business. Thousands of you come to Hollywood each year, searching for the magic lantern—and with you comes thousands upon thousands of dollars which go into the shops, the restaurants, the used car dealers, etc. It is pointless for anyone who has something to gain from you to dissuade your venturing to Tinsel Town. The terrors are never discussed, only the glamour.

You'd been told all the beautiful stories of the business you're contemplating, but none of the facts relative to what it's really like, and nothing to prepare you for what you should expect. My friend Criswell, famed for his television show and newspaper columns as "Criswell Predicts," predicted over two years ago that men would be letting their hair grow shoulder length or longer and would wear high-heeled shoes. How well we know this to have been proven out.

Turn on any "A Go-Go" show, or better still, walk down Hollywood Boulevard at anytime of the day or night. You can't tell the boys from the girls. They dress identically in their black

Capris, high-heeled boots, and mohair sweaters or colorful velour blouses (yes, I said blouses!).

Nothing is stranger than the strange itself. And there is no place else in the world stranger than my Tinsel Town of Hollywood. Almost everything seems to go! "It's my constitutional right to have purple hair if I want." Strange as it may seem, it probably is his constitutional right, but then, I'm no lawyer.

However, I do think a person has the right to choose how he wants to live, dress, find his way in life. But that doesn't give him carte blanche to the point where he won't find himself in trouble sooner or later. It is still the masses that control the patterns of our existence. The courts are blamed for all things, but the courts and the laws are designed by the demands of the multitudes. If you live as a beast, you become a beast.

CHAPTER TEN

How to Make a Cheap Picture and Fail

This is the easiest chapter of all to write! The first word to consider is film. Mr. Sleazy, the independent producer, and the major studios all pay the same to purchase the raw film stock. But after that everything changes. The same film you see used in a John Ford epic is the same film you see used in Mr. Sleazy's crap. What you finally see is what the producer does with the film. Either he makes an epic or he makes a mess.

Since I dealt with the sleaze producer in the last chapter, let's deal with the independent producer—we are not all good and certainly not all bad. I say we because I must classify myself and my associates as independent producers. Perhaps none of our films have, so far, been up for awards, but they are entertaining pictures. Our newly released *Orgy of the Dead* will be a pleasant surprise; it was filmed using a wide screen process and exciting color. It could well become a classic in its field. As well as enjoying the film, you might like to read my novel from which the screenplay was written. (It, too, is entitled *Orgy of the Dead*.)

Of course the legitimate, independent producer has been forced to change with the times also. We've had to use a certain amount of nudity along with realistic violence in our pictures. However, we try not to put in nudity just for nudity's sake. If nudity is used for ultraviolence, it has to mean something to the progression of the story. This is the same reasoning by which the major studios arrive at their decisions.

And it is not always an easy decision to come by. What may look excellent on paper becomes pretty crummy on the screen. By the same token, the reverse is true. From where I stood beside the camera watching a director with a series of dancers, they looked pretty bad, but when the film was shown, it turned out to be a classic of beauty and grace—a credit to the director, certainly not to the writer: me!

I guess the gods of luck have shined on me over the years. I have never made a film or been associated with a film that has not gone into release, generally with a major distributor. This is not always true for independents. There are millions of dollars' worth of film on laboratory shelves that will never see the light of the projection lamp, except when the producer screens something for his own enjoyment.

There are many reasons for this, and one of the most crucial is a history of bad deals. The independent producer very seldom gets a release for his picture in advance of production. The releasers very seldom will buy anything sight unseen. I was invited to a private screening by an important producer for several releasing companies, and as soon as the director's name appeared on the screen, all the releasers got up and left the room en masse. Each of them knew they would be seeing a badly directed picture because they knew the reputation of the director and that a picture of such low quality would be refused by even the sleaziest movie theaters. However, some stinkers do find their ways to the screen. In these cases it's all a matter of politics: who you know and how much you can grease the palm.

Of course, the story and cast are among the major causes for any film's failure. A weak story can never be strengthened by the best cast, and a strong story certainly is a failure if performed by a poor cast.

Many inexperienced producers take years to raise the money for their proposed productions. Then suddenly here they are with money and wasted months or years and they want to get started, so they grab the first story that comes along and a cast that has been passed along by others.

It's a great recipe for failure. By the same token, what in hell can any director do with a lousy cast and a rotten story? There was a film, in the days of 3-D, which only because it was 3-D, played the Paramount Theater in Hollywood (one of the major houses). The picture lasted one performance, then was scrapped until television came in. It claimed to be a science-fiction piece. The only science (or fiction) about it was the fact it came into being at all. And this so-called producer is still around Hollywood today taking backers' money for the same crap which never even gets the glory of one performance.

Another so-called producer has a unique way of distinguishing himself from his failures. My first experience with him was to write the pilot screenplay for a proposed television series for which I was never paid. But the guy had such a dynamic veneer you just liked to hear him talk. I guess this is the one attribute which has kept him in backers all these years, backers who put money into films which are never shown. It's an absolute fact; this character has made several films yet has never had one released. I'm outraged. Robbery, I call it, yet he never goes to jail.

He really does have plenty of imagination to pour into his sales pitch, only one day it really is going to kill him. Whenever he finds out his newest bad picture won't sell, he comes up with the damnedest strategy: suicide. In one instance, he sat on the roof of a hotel with a can of his film in his lap and his legs dangling over the street fifteen floors below, and then he gobbled down sleeping pills. Of course, the police had been conveniently notified, so they arrived in plenty of time.

In another try in reaction to the same movie, he stacked all the reels of his picture in the backseat of his car, then curled up with them, and permitted the carbon monoxide gas to enter the car via a hose. However again, the police had been alerted and were on the scene in plenty of time for his rescue. All his attempts at publicity were for naught. The stories were buried deep in the back pages of the newspapers and to this day the film has never been out of the can (shown on the screen). Every time these characters misuse some backers' money for their miserable projects, it means one less backer for the producer who is actually honest in his desire to make a good film and earn his backer a profit.

Money to produce movies is not easy to come by under any circumstances.

When I decided to produce *Plan 9 from Outer Space* (at that time it was called *Grave Robbers from Outer Space*), I assembled the best I ever had. There was Criswell, Lyle Talbot, Tom Keene, Mona McKinnon, Vampira "Queen of the Horror Movies," Gregory Walcott, Bud Osborne, Dudley Manlove, Paul Marco, Ben Frommer, David De Mering, Duke Moore, and the famous Hollywood monster man Tor Johnson! And Bela Lugosi, in his final film.

Bela died months before I started this production, but we had made several thousand feet of film in advance. Producers often shoot some footage of the star to help him sell the picture to backers.

My backers turned out to be several ministers and preachers of the Southern Baptist Church. They were interested in doing this film because a horror picture always makes money, and they needed money to make a series of religious movies. As negotiations progressed, they felt that the stars and I should attend church more often––their church. After Tor Johnson and I had attended a few Sundays (and remember, there was only the promise of money, nothing solidified), it was suggested that we join the Baptist church.

Now this is going all out for your movie money. Tor and I walked up the aisle and declared our intentions: we vowed to join! At the time, Tor weighed in the neighborhood of four-hundred-twelve pounds. The church informed us that we would have to be baptized, which consisted of being completely submerged in "blessed" water on stage in front of a congregation. This immediately presented a tremendous problem: Tor's tremendous size. The church just didn't have a tub big enough.

It was decided the only thing big enough for dunking the giant wrestler-turned-actor was a swimming pool. One Sunday morning, the church services convened early. Tor and I, with the lovely young lady Kathy O'Hara, were taken by limousine to a swimming pool in Beverly Hills, with the entire congregation following in their Bentleys, Rolls Royces, and Jaguars. I got the strange feeling of being in the lead car in a funeral procession.

Eventually, however, the pool was blessed, the services began, and Tor and I were dunked. Tor, an Olympic-level swimmer even with his great bulk, decided that on the third dunking, he would fall out of the aged preacher's hands and pretend he couldn't swim.

He frightened not only the preacher who couldn't possibly lift him, but the entire assembled congregation. Always the showman, Tor allowed the suspense long enough for the drama to build, then swam away. Certainly we all play the game to get the money to make our pictures. If you believe my tale is a stretch of the imagination—the product of a writer's imagination—the facts are on file with the church in Beverly Hills.

I've also had to ride horses (and I'm no rider); I've dived from a three-story building into four feet of water (and I'm an excellent diver); I've raced cars, played poker, and fallen from stagecoaches. I've been lucky. None of my films have been left on the laboratory shelf.

I've lived the Hollywood rat race and I've filmed in the Hollywood rat race. Check my films! And check some others! And then realize how easy it is to make a cheap picture and fail.

CHAPTER ELEVEN

The Young One

There is a young lady, just outside of Montreal, Canada, who read one of my articles a few years ago and has been my constant penpal ever since.

She read what I wrote and took a liking to what I was saying. She stayed home to complete her schooling and to study drama at a good program. She is growing into her varied talents.

I can say here that Micheline Senecal is the smart one and when finally she is ready and does come to Hollywood, I will be in a position to help her. One important thing—she will not have to face the Hollywood rat race the way I see it.

CHAPTER TWELVE

So You
Want to Be a Writer

Somewhere along here, I figure it's time to say something about the writer. All of you are not aspiring to be actors or actresses. Some of you, I'm sure, have other fields of endeavor in mind. I class myself in the category of writer, and so do many of you. I don't know who said it, but there is an adage "Everyone has at least one book in them." In some people, it is stronger than in others. Get used to the idea early: writing is a stormy career. One day you've got a publisher and the next day you haven't. That's about the time the department of water and power steps in and turns off your water and electricity. And if you work on an electric typewriter as I do, you're out of business.

Like acting, writing is a business. But it isn't every morning you get up, sit down with the old pencil and paper, and the greatest ideas in the world flow. More often you will sit down and the blank sheet of paper will stare right back at you. An angry slab challenging every thought you might have. A white glob stifling every urge. But this is the monster you must conquer. And once you've accomplished something, read it over and see if you like what you have written. Then rip it up. Start over again.

Writing is a business and it takes time. In most cases, it's years before you see your first words in print. Even though I had many screenplays to my credit, but there was always, in the back of my mind, the novel, the book, the printed word. When I began my writing for novels, a publisher said to me, "Sure, you're a good screenwriter—but screenwriters don't really make very good novelists." This is a strange remark since many screenwriters have turned out very good novels, even prize-winning novels heralded around the world. But that is part of the same old merry-go-round, as actors and actresses find. Show me! Then comes another of the same old routines: work your heart out for two-hundred pages on something you really believe is good, then see if the same publisher will even look at it.

Even after nine novels, an associate editor of a company that had published most of them didn't know who I was. Finally, I was able to convince him I was not the beginner he took me for and he asked me to write a book with a certain type of character. I did. It was a simple novel, but it took me a little more than a month. My original editor returned from his leave and rejected it. Not suitable. There went more than a month of work down the drain—a month I could have devoted my attention to things that would have paid off. The telephone company doesn't wait. The gas company has a collection agency. Fortunately the water and power company turn-offs have only been a day or two between checks. Eventually, the novel did sell to another company.

Nothing comes easily, particularly inspiration. I guess I've been asked a few hundred times, "Where do you get your ideas?"

It's not an easy question to answer. Ideas come from many sources. I even keep a pencil and pad beside my bed at night because many a dream turns out to be a good plot. That's where *Bride of the Monster* came from, although it was first called *Bride of the Atom*. *Final Curtain*, which was not only a half-hour television show but was later turned into my novel *Orgy of the Dead*, came to me while I was going to drama school in Washington, DC (Oh yes! I also went through the drama school bit). I lived in an atticlike affair over a theater, and there is nothing more spooky than a theater after hours. Every sound is magnified hundreds of times. Picture yourself in a gigantic building, there is no one there but you, and it's very dark. I can guarantee the imagination will start to percolate with enough ideas for a lifetime. Of course I don't advocate locking yourself in a dark attic just to get ideas. You might end up stark raving mad in the rubber room at the happy farm. Ideas are all around you: "Seek and ye shall find."

The main idea is to keep writing. No matter what it is. Keep at it because even if your story gets worse, you will be getting better. You'll sit and dream most of the time, but you must first conquer the big white glob with the typewriter imprints.

If you are going to be a writer, you must be prepared to handle any job that comes your way. No one can teach you to write. You either can or you can't. Oh, I suppose a certain command of the language is advisable; however, usage of words all over the world is changing every day and new words are being added. There is even a new dictionary defining words that have been invented in the past twenty years. A writer must keep up with the times. Because I write so many spooky stories, my desk has an encyclopedia of occultism. Such books are as much a part of your working tools as pencil, paper, and typewriter.

Speaking of your typewriter, keep the keys clean and brush them often with a stiff typewriter brush. There is nothing more off-putting to a publisher than a sloppy manuscript. He's liable not to look beyond the first page. You don't sell stories that way.

Although I detest synopsis writing because I don't feel I can tell my story that way, it is the general rule that publishers to want to see the first chapter and a few pages of synopsis for the rest. But let's not knock it! Many a great story has been sold in this fashion. I just don't happen to write that way. However, there is something to say for establishing yourself with certain publishers and studios. You have a much larger scope in submitting or even getting commissioned assignments.

Today, your first sale is likely going to be in the field of paperbacks. Paperback novels use up more material each month than television. Think of the great many newsstands, drug stores, and supermarkets in your own hometown that display the hundreds of titles each month. Then multiply that by all the places all over the world, and you'll get some idea how great this market is. Most of these places change their titles each month or two—it's a vast, consuming market. In most cases, it doesn't take an overwhelming talent to write these books and sell them.

The majority of paperback novels are about sex or action adventure. Fast-packed action and fast-paced characters. Most run from one-hundred-sixty to one-hundred-ninety-five pages, or forty-thousand to sixty-thousand words. And they need climax after climax, with a power-packed ending.

Don't expect to get rich in this market. Paperback publishers pay anywhere from two-hundred-fifty dollars to seven-hundred-fifty dollars for first rights. But then, there are many motion picture companies that don't pay much more for a screenplay, and although it takes much more time to write one and much more thought.

The adage about screenwriters may be true in reverse. The writer of a screenplay must always think in the present, "He walks across the room. She takes him in her arms." The novel would read, "He walked across the room and she took him in her arms."

The same is true for dialogue. The novel would read, "He walked across the room and she took him in her arms. His eyes looked deep into hers as he softly spoke into her ear, 'My darling!' Then with endearment he continued, 'There is no one in the world but you!'"

The screenplay it would look like this:

```
21   INT. LIVING ROOM - MEDIUM SHOT - PANNING - NIGHT
     Joe walks across the room (CAMERA PANNING) and Mary
     takes him into her arms. They look deeply into each
     other's eyes. He puts his lips close to her ear.

                         JOE
                         (softly)
                         "My darling!"
                         (endearment)
                         "There is no one in the world but
                         you!"

     They lock into a tender embrace for the. . . .
                         FADE OUT.
```

There are other variations for television scripts and certainly for radio, but the format can be found in any textbook.

Writing fiction is great fun. It's much like God creating his world and his people, putting them in a situation, then directing their every movement. You develop the situation to a point where all comes out right or wrong, as you choose. I must admit I've never known where my stories are going. The idea starts and along the way, characters become involved and *develop*—the key word is *develop*. I've never, for instance, known an ending to my own stories and it's more fun. The characters just take over, and I become only an instrument through which they exist. I believe this is one of the most important aspects to any story. If your characters don't live, they can't possibly be believable. They must live their own lives and reap their own destinies.

A case in point is my own *Grave Robbers from Outer Space*, the last film in which Bela Lugosi appeared. We had been shooting eight days on a twelve-day schedule before I came up with the ending. After all, in the screenplay I had already given my audience space-ships, a space war, weird people, supersonic grave robbers, and the destruction of Hollywood. Where was the topper? Kathy and I found one, and that's where the Solarnite Bomb came into being: a bomb that could ignite the actual particles of sunlight and could touch off an explosion anywhere with sunlight in the universe. Not a cliff hanger, which all action stories should have, but the final topper, which is greater than all the others. The impact should remembered right up until the time of your next book or movie. "You're only as good as your last one!"

Never overlook any form of writing. I'd just finished writing and directing an independent production called *The Sinister Urge*, when the studio head came to me and asked if I'd consider writing some documentary films connected with the government aircraft industries. I'd never been called on for that type of assignment before since

I'm foremost a fiction writer. But it was an interesting challenge and if you are a writer and you know the facts, you can write anything. The only thing that bothered me—for certainly the money was good—was the possibility of boredom. Writing about nuts and bolts didn't seem very romantic to me. But the twenty-eight weeks with Autonetics, a division of North American Aircraft, turned out to be a pleasure I will remember the rest of my life.

I wasn't writing about nuts and bolts. After getting government clearances, I was in on the takeoff of the first Minute Man missile. Then came a trip aboard the USS *Oklahoma* for stories of her sextant chronometers, radarscope, and radio compass. And I did an article on the space capsule even before the public had any inkling of its existence.

It turned out to be better than fiction. One of the most interesting things I've gotten to do was direct live television at a spacecraft construction plant. The point was to describe the dust-free area to the employees. The dust-free zone is kept entirely clean of dirt because the slightest particle of dust could foul up the delicate instruments of the rockets and their guidance systems. Everyone wears nylon coats and hats—that never go beyond the sealed-in area—much like doctors. To enter, we had to pass through wind and suction machines that actually pull every last particle of dust from your body, like a shoe shine by large, rotating brushes. Even your hair gets mussed up thoroughly in the suction machine—a great way to get rid of dandruff. Our cameras, lights, even my clipboard, paper, and pencil got special treatment in that wind tunnel. Stories are all around you, if you just keep your eyes open.

After completing my screenplay *Orgy of the Dead,* I decided to branch out in my writing. This time I tried my hand at political writing. I had been interested in doing this for a long time, but then came the proper moment. I connected with the reelection campaign for the fine mayor of Los Angeles, Sam Yorty. He was reelected by a tremendous margin, and I like to think my words—and there were thousands of them—did much to help.

Writing is fun, but a difficult job all the same. Although the market for all types of writing expands with every passing year, it also becomes more exacting. Material sold to television five years ago couldn't possibly get beyond a front-office secretary today. If you doubt it, look at some of the morning and afternoon reruns, then watch the prime-time shows in the evening. Match one against the other: the characters are much more defined in the recent shows and the plots are much more involved. Take the simple Western of the 1930s. It's almost impossible, even with a petition signed by thousands of names, to get one on the Saturday morning kiddie shows. Unless the hero wears a black hat and dirty clothes, rides a black horse, rapes his leading lady, and visits his psychiatrist once a week "it just ain't got it!"

Don't write a doctor story unless you have a medical degree or a giant medical dictionary—and even then only if you can come up with the rarest disease only known to the lost tribes of the Incas and its cure (a medicine derived from an almost extinct reptile found under a rock in a lost treasure chest off the coast of Japan). This may sound ridiculous, but you know those shows.

Much writing that sells is ridiculous. I think even writers will admit that. But if you want to write what sells, you need to write what the public wants to read. It's nothing new. You never make money by being a martyr, or tilting at windmills, because few want to read such things. And the few who do, don't pay the bills.

Newspaper writers are not the best paid writers in the world, but at least they are writing. In the back of all journalists' minds is the thought of writing the Great American Novel. Some do it, others take so much time away from the job they are being paid to do that they end up on the street looking for another job simply to pay the rent. Or as some skid-row inhabitants could tell you, trying to get enough for their next bottle of cheap wine. So let's not start out to write the Great Novel—just be a writer who writes. Be content with just being a writer.

If you want to be a writer and can make a living at it—in whatever field of writing it may be— you are a writer in an honest profession and doing a necessary job. Every business and every pleasure under the sun requires the services of a writer.

It's terrible to me to hear someone say about someone else's work, "Ahh, that stinks!" Yet the critic probably couldn't ink his way out of a paper bag. You put it on paper. Good, bad, or indifferent. At least you had the guts to put it there.

It is said that D. W. Griffith wanted to write a stage play his whole life. He started as a young man and he was still working on it the day he died. The man was a talented and gifted producer and director, but he wanted to be a writer. I doubt if the world will ever see his efforts as a playwright. Everyone who wants to be a writer, no matter how successful he might be in other fields—even allied fields—doesn't necessarily make it. It's a tough row to hoe at best. Come to think of it, why don't you give it up before you get started? And that's not sour grapes! That's good, sound advice, which few of you will take . . . but sound advice all the same.

If the drama bug has bitten you, and the writing wing of that bug has dug in the deepest, you have the right to try. Most will fall by the wayside but the few who really have guts, determination, and purpose will succeed. A few will achieve greatness. The remainder will become members of that grand and honored society called "writers."

With respect to all of my fellow writers, I must hasten to add that we cannot live forever, and we cannot furnish the world with all its writing needs. Somewhere along the line the new writer must be developed, and if we can aid, we should be prepared to do so. In the long run, it can do nothing but help us.

Nothing stays the same. In my father's lifetime he has experienced the horse as his only transportation; and indeed he rode one to school, summer and winter. God willing, he will live to see the first man on the moon four years from now. That's a long span, from horse to automobile, to airplane, to rocket, to spaceship, with a few wars in between.

Take advantage of the advances of the last seventy years and apply these drastic changes to your work. I never know from one morning to the next if the same words I've used for years will even have the same meaning. Possibly a week from now there will be yet another dictionary with more new words, usages, and changes. I am a writer for money—I do nothing else for a living but write. So if a new dictionary or thesaurus comes out, I'll get it. It's all tax deductible, and these are the tools of my trade.

I must also classify changes as tools of my trade, and I must be ready to accept them, even if changing times are not tax deductible.

So you want to be a writer? OK. Be one.

CHAPTER THIRTEEN

Hollywood

Exactly what can I say about Hollywood? I've resided here for many years and there is everything here from good to bad. You must have both anywhere, because you must have the bad to evaluate the good. But Hollywood is not just anywhere—it has been called the entertainment capital of the world. Hollywood *is* more controversial.

All the travel folders boast of the great hotels and the theaters. Take them as you see them, they are all here, just as the travel folders depict. The only problem is the travel folders photos are dated—most of those pictures were taken years ago when stars actually did walk along Hollywood Boulevard. At the time when Hollywood really was the entertainment capital of the world. You might have seen Buck Jones and his horse Silver, or Tom Mix and Tony, John Barrymore, Tom Keene, Herbert Rawlinson, Francis X. Bushman, and all the others, a kaleidoscope of stars riding in the annual Thanksgiving Parade.

I was privileged to see such a parade. It was just after World War II. Almost every car in the long procession had a movie star in it. Stars I had seen on the screen and loved for years. I remember distinctly Hopalong Cassidy astride his white horse Topper and Wallace Beery. They had always been such favorites.

Of course, the Thanksgiving Parade still exists and the Rose Parade is of national interest. But these events are no longer the jewels of the entertainment capital of the world. Today, one or perhaps two stars may consent to appear. The floats are embellished with lovely girls, but who are they? Where did they come from and where do they go? Who knows them except for a few close friends and perhaps the politicians who got them rides on the float in the first place? They are apparently starlets, but starlets of what? For what? In what? Who really wants to have their time wasted on such a farce? It seems to me it's easy to see why the real stars no longer turn out for such events, just as they no longer turn out on the Sunset Strip or many of the other places they once frequented.

A star donates his or her time to participate in such events because he or she expects to see and be seen. Since these events have become overrun with little girls next door, all dressed up in frilly white dresses in cars with little-known politicians, why indeed should the star waste his time? Most of the crowd has turned away in boredom before the star even gets his chance to be seen.

The Rose Parade and the Thanksgiving Parade—or as it is more popularly known, the Santa Claus Lane Parade—are the only two so-called big parades in the Los Angeles area. I wonder if it wouldn't bring back much of the glamour if there were fewer girls next door and fewer local politicians and their wives. Of course, many of you reading this are the little girls next door and you may resent what I am saying. But put yourself in the stars' place. Would you like a bunch of kids like you cluttering up the day? Next comes the long line of inevitably very bad high school bands.

I have long since given up attending these parades. Why stand around in the cold getting bored when I can endure the same boredom at home watching television with a whiskey in my hand? And when the announcer gives the name, rank, and serial number of someone in the next flower-draped automobile, furnished for the event by one or more Hollywood automotive dealers, I can say, "Who'd he say?" and be comfortable about it. Television is a remarkable invention.

The next event of by-gone days is the Hollywood premiere. Today we have bigger and better movies than ever before. The movie screen has grown in size to match the gigantic scope of the films themselves. Not long ago I drove to Disneyland. I stood in the middle of one of the exhibits and saw an entire circle of moving pictures projected around me. It was as if I were driving a car and I saw exactly the landscape I'd see in reality. Movies are definitely bigger, better, and steadily gaining in sophistication. Yet the premiere of today is probably the most slipshod affair imaginable. It mocks the meaning of the privilege of filmmaking and the glamour it was created to promote. Because of television, it is seen by more people than ever before, yet there is precious little to see.

Once upon a time—as tales used to begin—the premiere was star-studded. Nearly every big star in Hollywood attended, no matter which studio held their contract. Watch the old newsreels and see for yourself. The premiere was a gala night to be remembered by all—stars and public alike. It was most enjoyable to see a Humphrey Bogart, James Cagney, Marlene Dietrich, Madeleine Carroll, Katharine Hepburn, Spencer Tracy, even Tom Mix, and so many more, all assembled in their finery, gathered in front of the kleig lights before entering Gruman's Chinese or the Egyptian theater. And the fans were there, in droves, cheering them on, to catch a glimpse, maybe with luck a hello and an autograph. On those rare occasions, the stars had come out of their ivory castles to be seen by the people. And those male stars were always accompanied by female stars—known names, known faces. They were each and all a part of themselves. Apart from the world. Perhaps the height of star status is what made them the greats and made everyone want to pay their money at the box office.

Today the premiere appears to be the same hodgepodge of nonentities as the parades. Even the announcers must refer to their notes most of the time and then stammer over the names of those who come before the television cameras. It's strictly a smattering of people in tuxedos and evening dresses who have paid some fantastic price in the name of sweet charity, to be seen at such events. Elderly men with young and beautiful girls trying to prove they can still hook the young ones.

If the producers can get one or two of the actors to attend the premiere, they are lucky. Truthfully, thinking as the actor might, who needs it? The actor has done the job, so why should the star embarrass himself by violating his privacy to see a film he's already seen, to be subjected to a bunch of people not remotely connected with the business, and to be placed in front of a television camera, most likely after the viewer has gone to sleep. It's the star's picture yet the star has been thrown into second, third, or even last place at his own gala event.

It's no wonder the entertainment capital of the world has become just another place like any other place. Actually, there is no Hollywood any longer. It's become a kaleidoscope of meaningless ectoplasms which abound between reality and the unreality. This is not altogether the fault of the studio and its executives, or the independent studio and its executives. Perhaps the fault lies in the star system itself. Except for the remaining stars of the 1930s, there are no stars of today. Someone new comes to the surface in a television series and lives for the length of a series—long or short— then passes into eternity. A few try other series if the network moguls give them a second chance. But it never works. Perhaps they are so typecast that a new character doesn't come across. In the 1930s and 1940s, the star was cast in many varied roles. One day he was a cowboy, the next a lover, the next a detective. The young fellow or girl of today when cast in a television series plays the same character week in and week out. It's no wonder the mind of the public can't accept him or her in something else. Often the star of a series that endures is one who reigned supreme in the movies. These stars earned respect by putting in years of hard work and devotion to their art.

I'm going to repeat my earlier advice: stay home. That's exactly what you should do. You can be a devoted actor or actress there as well as any place. One look at Hollywood Boulevard and your dedication might well fly out of the window. You're just as close to Hollywood as your nearest airfield . . . and you're closer to the inside of a studio at home than if you were standing at Hollywood and Vine.

Years ago, Hollywood Boulevard was a show street. Today, it's just another street of stores, some more fancy than others, but nothing you couldn't find on your own main street. The sidewalks do have bronze plaques with the names of stars, but you want more than a life of walking with your head down reading names!

Sunset Boulevard is a big nothing. Where once the great nightclubs abounded, there are only small bistros where the "in" set gathers, where it's difficult to tell the girls from the boys between the beatniks and the long-hairs. Precious few have even had interviews—it would seem they have all come to Hollywood with guitars. Today everybody's a singer. Or professes to be. Fortunately much of their guitar twanging and nasal dripping is confined to cheap joints called "coffee houses." Each Friday and Saturday night they converge with the police, who make their quota of arrests for all types of disturbances. Ironically, the greatest show place on the Sunset Strip happens to be owned by a great guitarist and singer. It's Gene Autry and his Hotel Continental.

Where once was the Trocadaro, the Macombo, the Parisian, Allah's Gardens, and Ciro's—clubs where the stars gathered— there now stand banks and other institutions of lesser learning. Is it any wonder the stars no longer drive up in their big cars to visit a coffee house? They'd be out of their minds and probably be taking their lives in their hands.

The city fathers, the Chamber of Commerce, the councilmen and civic beautification organizations are trying to do something to improve Hollywood's glamour rating, but it takes a long time. Recently an organization planted a few trees along Hollywood Boulevard, but it will take many years before any one of those trees gives shade to the midget who touts the Hollywood Wax Museum, which by the way is a very fine show.

Vine Street is the only other noteworthy street in Hollywood. You have heard the name—it's where the Brown Derby is, which is about the only building that retains its character over the years. The famed Criswell and I go there often. I'd say the Brown Derby is the only place left where industry people are still respected.

But that's the extent of it. That's the Hollywood as an insider knows it. Trouble. Problems. Heartaches . . .

Believe it or not, your life is more real than the Hollywood scene.